READY-MADE
INVESTING

READY-MADE INVESTING

FOR BUSY YOUNG PROFESSIONALS – TAKING THE WORRY OUT OF MANAGING YOUR MONEY

WALTER COXON

Matador
Unit E2 Airfield Business Park,
Harrison Road, Market Harborough,
Leicestershire. LE16 7UL
Tel: 0116 2792299
Email: books@troubador.co.uk
Web: www.troubador.co.uk/matador
Twitter: @matadorbooks

ISBN 978 1803132 020

Cover artwork by Lauren Christian

British Library Cataloguing in Publication Data.
A catalogue record for this book is available from the British Library.

Printed and bound in Great Britain by 4edge Limited
Typeset in 11pt Minion Pro by Troubador Publishing Ltd, Leicester, UK

Matador is an imprint of Troubador Publishing Ltd

Disclaimer:
While I have worked in the wealth and investments field for a long time, I am
not a qualified financial adviser. Even if I were, I would not be able to advise you
without knowing your particular circumstances. The facts in this book are true to the
best of my knowledge and belief but there may be mistakes or there may have been
changes since publication, so please check the facts for yourself before taking any action.
I will not be liable for any loss, of any kind, that you incur as a result of making
investment decisions based on the information in this book.

For Kathryn, David & Rachel

CONTENTS

WHY I WROTE THIS BOOK

My eldest daughter told me one day that her friends were asking her advice on money matters, on the basis they worked out she knew things they didn't, because they knew she had a dad who knew about these things. So, she said I should write a book for people like her friends, who don't have ready access to a dad (or mum) who knows these things. A couple of years on, I did that and here it is!

My eldest daughter was born in 1996, which I believe puts her on the borderline of Gen Z and Millennial (her younger sister has been known to declare with disdain – "*that's such a millennial attitude.*"). I also have a son who is 15 months younger. Both my eldest daughter and my son have recently started into the world of work. I have written this book with their age group in mind; people who are just starting out on their investing journey. They may want to be financially independent at a young age and have the freedom to downshift to a different, less remunerative career. Or, more immediately, it may be simply the need to understand what their employer pension plans do. Or wanting to build up a nest egg to buy a house. And they need to start establishing the right habits so they can reduce the stress that seems to hover around money for so many people.

I am not a qualified financial advisor. But this is my patch. I have worked in and around financial services for 20 years. Most of that time I worked in a wealth management firm that provided fully-advised services and online services for DIY investors. I have been a trustee, I have been a member of an investment committee, I have been on the board of a regulated investment firm, and I have designed wealth management market strategies and implemented new business offerings.

This book is not advice. As you will learn as you read further, proper financial advice needs to be personal and given in the context of a comprehensive understanding of your circumstances. But this is me sharing my knowledge as a 'local', showing you around my patch and explaining how I believe you should navigate the world of investments.

Philosophically I think things need to be kept simple. Life is too full and busy for unnecessary complexity. So that thread runs through this book. I am the sort of person who likes to set things on autopilot, who doesn't like the idea of spending hours each week fiddling with my portfolio. My budget arrangements must be basic; I can't be bothered with writing every expense on a list or in an app and reconciling it all every month. And I think most people are the same. If it is too complicated or burdensome it won't happen, or it will happen for a while and then will fall apart. But I am also not one of those people who just pays someone to sort things out for me. I want to be sure I get a good deal, and I am happy to put in a bit of time up front to make sure I set things up the right way.

So that's why this book is focused on 'ready-made' investing. It is for people with busy lives who don't have time to faff with their investments. But it is also for people who want to be sure they get a good deal and don't pay any more than they need to, who want to make sure they keep the costs of investing as low as is sensible and have more of their hard-earned cash going into their investments.

WHY YOU SHOULD
READ THIS BOOK

We all know that we need to save and invest so we can put together the deposit on that house, for financial independence or to fund our retirement.

We know that cash is not an investment, interest rates are pitiful, and inflation eats away at your savings, so we have to take on some risk and invest in the stock market, if we want our money to grow for the long term.

And for retirement savings the stakes are higher. Where the previous generation typically had a 'defined benefit' or final salary pension where they got paid a guaranteed inflation-linked pension in retirement, most of us now have to save into a 'defined contribution' plan, where, if we don't save enough or we invest it badly, we face penury in our retirement.

The world of investing can appear frighteningly complex; an impenetrable fog of jargon and riddled with costly traps for the unwary.

To the uninitiated there seem to be just two unpalatable choices to success in this world:

1. You need deep knowledge of the markets, and to dedicate hours each week if you want to do this yourself, or
2. You need to find a good and trustworthy advisor, which is not easy to do if you don't have a lot of money.

But it is not true that this is difficult to do yourself, or that doing this yourself takes a vast amount of time. The key is investing in a 'ready-made' investment portfolio, where someone else has done the hard work of working out the right blend of investments.

If you had an advisor, chances are this is essentially what they would advise you to do anyway. Surprisingly, most advisor or wealth management firms have a very small number of 'ready-made' portfolios (typically around five), ranging from 'conservative' to 'adventurous growth' and they will identify which one is right for you and invest all your money in that one portfolio and just leave it there.

Of course, you also need to make sure you take advantage of the tax breaks the government gives and make sure your investments are via tax efficient pensions and ISA wrappers.

Also, you need to keep your costs low, saving money on fees so you maximise the return on your hard-earned savings. And by doing this yourself and investing directly in a low-cost ready-made fund, you really save on fees.

Once this is done there is no need for constant tinkering; just keep investing so you put aside enough and stick with the plan through good markets and bad ones. And sticking with the plan is often the hardest part.

There are a lot of books out there on investing, and many of them are very interesting to some of us. But most of them won't help the non-investment professional to do what they need to do to save and invest to reach their goals.

In this book I will explain this all to you so you will understand what you should do and then I will show you how to do it step by step.

Hopefully you realise there is no magic way to getting rich quickly. But if you follow the guidance in this book you will build up your wealth, slowly. But this isn't about being wealthy. It is about having a plan, being in control of your money, making sure that your finances don't cause unnecessary stress and make you unhappy and making sure you can fund your plan, whether that's a deposit on that house, for financial independence or to fund your retirement.

Finally, you will notice this book is short. That's because (a) it is really not that complicated and (b) I want to be sure you will read it all the way to the end!

INTRODUCTION

So why should you save and invest? For many it is to put together the deposit on that house, for others it's to have some capital to start a business, or for financial independence or to fund retirement.

For retirement savings the stakes are high. The 'full' state pension is only £185.15[1] a week and if you don't save or you invest badly, you face penury in retirement.

What would a financial advisor recommend you do, if you had one (or could afford one)? Yes, they would tell you to invest, put aside money for the future. But how would they advise you to go about investing?

Encouragingly they will all pretty much tell you about the same things:

1. You are going to need to take on some risk (i.e., the chance you will lose some of your money) – there is no reward without risk and that means some stock market shares or funds of shares in your portfolio (and cash is not an investment).

2. Diversify your investments (i.e., don't put all your eggs in one basket) by investing in a 'multi-asset' portfolio.
3. Take advantage of the tax breaks and incentives and put your investments in an ISA and/or a pension.
4. Invest enough; and
5. Stick with it (through the market ups and downs).

Actually, persuading you to 'stick with it' is something that the better advisors will focus on. Once you have set up the plan and understand what you are doing you may feel you don't need an advisor. However, many of us struggle with 'composure' – the ability to stick with the plan, even when the markets are going down.

Carl Richards, creator of the *Sketch Guy*, a *New York Times* column in which he explains financial concepts in just a few strokes of a marker pen, has this cautionary illustration on the cover of his book, *The Behavior Gap*.

Figure 1: Fear and Greed

I often think that the most important role an advisor plays is to make sure you stick with the plan and talk you out of selling down when the markets are a bit choppy. It is a bit like having a personal trainer; yes, they show you how to exercise properly, but for most of us the real value is in the structure and discipline; they keep you at it and work you a bit harder than you would on your own. Like with exercise, often the right thing to do is the most uncomfortable, and we need help to push through.

The thing that will most surprise those who are new to the world of investing, is the extent to which financial advisors invest most of their clients' assets in just a very small number of 'ready-made' model portfolios or funds and each client is typically invested in just one of these. Advisors don't spend a great deal of time building and tailoring investment portfolios for their clients (though a few will try and pretend they do). They pick a good fund or portfolio manager (or employ one themselves) who has done the hard work of building a set of well-diversified ready-made portfolios[2] and use one of perhaps five risk variants of these ready-made portfolios for each of their clients. In fact, ready-made portfolios were constructed by asset managers with the express objective of making financial advisors' lives easier. They offer advisors simple, quick solutions to meeting their client needs, freeing up their time to build their business and attract new clients.

The great thing is this makes it really simple for you to do the same thing for yourself. I will show you in Chapter 7 the most popular funds of ready-made portfolios used by financial advisors across the UK, and how as a DIY investor you can invest as an advisor would tell you to. Or if you want to make it even easier for yourself, you can use a 'robo-advisor', where you are guided through a series of steps on a mobile app or online to invest in the right diversified fund for you. I will explain what robo-advisors do and help you choose one if you decide you need a little more help and that's the route you want to go.

By following this approach yourself, you will save money on fees. A DIY investor can invest for total fees of less than 0.5% of assets for a 'passive' portfolio (more on 'passive' vs 'active' later). A robo-advisor typically costs around 1% for the same portfolio. A fully advised service with a real person as an advisor will cost you 2% or more. That may not sound much, but when your portfolio is only delivering 4 or 5% after inflation, you could be using half of what you make on your investments to pay advice and management fees. Over many years, this can cost you a very significant proportion of your investment pot – over 20 years a 1.5% difference in fees will end up costing a third of your portfolio.

You may think this is too complicated to do yourself or will take too much time. The financial services industry often appears to speak a language of its own that's unintelligible to outsiders. In these pages I will lead you through the key concepts and hope to show you that it is really not that complicated and that it shouldn't take a lot of time. I am going to show you how to invest as an advisor would recommend you to. Advisors don't spend hours every week tinkering with each of their client's portfolios. No, they invest their clients in well-diversified ready-made portfolios built by professional, experienced and reputable portfolio managers. You can do this too.

While it is great to have an advisor help you through the investment process and to provide a reassuring voice when the markets are choppy, they are expensive. You can do this yourself and save a lot of money by doing so. Also, very few are interested in helping the 'smaller' clients (i.e., with less than £50,000– £100,000 to invest), and those that do are even more expensive.

To give you an idea of how expensive they can be, there was an article in the *Financial Times* in September 2019 entitled *Lloyds-Schroders wealth management venture to launch price war*[3]. The report claimed that Schroders had estimated that customers of St James's Place (SJP, one of the UK's largest wealth managers) pay 7.95% of their investment in the first year, compared with 4.7% with Brewin Dolphin (another large wealth manager) and 'only' 3.65% with Schroders. Subsequent years' fees were estimated at 2.95% for SJP, 2.7% for Brewin Dolphin and 'only' 1.9% for Schroders. SJP disputed the quoted fees in its response to the report but did not provide a corrected estimate. Prices have since come down a bit – looking at the website at the time of writing for these three providers shows that for a portfolio under £500,000 first year fees[4] could still be between 3.5% (Schroder's) and around 7% (SJP) and ongoing fees will still be at least 1.75% (Schroders) and over 2% if you choose one of the other two firms. This, all for a service that you could do yourself for less than 0.5% and achieve the same (or possibly better) investment performance.

Yes, there are things that you need financial planning advice for. For example, for good reason, certain types of pension transfers are not permitted unless you have taken advice. There may also be value in getting one-off advice to check over your financial plans. The key is to ensure you pay for this planning advice on a one-off basis and don't get drawn into long-term ongoing advisor fees. You could do this when there is a significant event, such as coming into an inheritance or transferring or consolidating your pensions from employment. In Chapter 5 I'll talk you through the situations where it may make sense to use an advisor and how to find one.

The key is to have your money working for you and not for your advisor or fund manager. If you pay high fees, it could well be that the professionals are making a better return on your portfolio than you are. There is a classic investment book written in 1940 with the title *Where are the customers' yachts?*[5]. The title refers to a story of a visitor to New York who admired the yachts of the bankers and brokers moored up in the harbour and naively asked his companion where the customers' yachts were. Of course, in the story there weren't any – there was more money to be made in the giving of the advice than in taking it.

Future returns for a well-balanced portfolio are unlikely to be much more than 4–5% after inflation. If your financial advisor is taking 3% of that then there isn't much left for you. And you can do this yourself and your costs will be less than 0.5%, leaving most of that return intact, growing your wealth year on year. Over time the effect of compounding this difference in costs makes a huge difference to the size of your portfolio. This is illustrated in Figure 2 with a portfolio returning 5%. If you invest £10,000 as a lump sum, with fees at 0.5%, after 30 years your portfolio will be worth over £37,000. With fees of 3% it will be worth less than half that, around £18,000, with the rest of the value going to your advisors and/or fund managers.

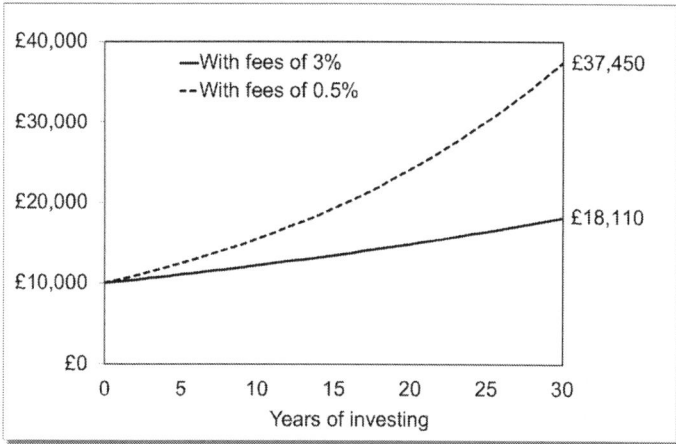

Figure 2: The true cost of fees to your portfolio

In summary:

- You need to take on some risk – there is no reward without risk.
- Diversify your investment ('don't put all your eggs in one basket'), by investing in a 'ready-made' portfolio comprising shares and bonds from different sectors and geographies.
- Take advantage of the tax breaks and government incentives to save by putting your investments in an ISA/LISA and/or pension.
- Keep costs low; by doing this yourself you will minimise costs.
- Make sure you set up a plan to save enough; and
- Stick with the plan through the market ups and downs.

1

RISK AND RETURN

AND WHY YOU HAVE TO TAKE SOME RISKS

In this chapter, I am going to explain what investment risk is, why you need to take on some risk to make higher returns and how to understand how much risk it is right for you to take on – your risk tolerance.

Cash is not an investment, and you should not leave long-term money in cash. Of course, you need some cash; for spending in the near term, or in a rainy-day account for unexpected expenses. Cash is the most 'liquid' asset – it is there ready to use and you don't have to sell something to get it. Also, there is no risk of it losing its 'nominal' value. But every year inflation eats away at its value and the interest you earn is pitiful. Think of a grandparent finding a £50 note in an envelope at the back of a bookshelf that was put away for safekeeping in the 1960s. At the time it may well have been a couple of weeks' wages and paid for their entire month's rent leaving some change for food. At today's prices £50 won't pay for more than a few days' rent in most parts of Britain. The 'nominal' value of the note is still

£50, but inflation has ravaged its buying power. Yes, with cash you don't have the risk of your savings losing some of its value in a market crash. But that's because it is already losing money every year.

Warren Buffett, the legendary investor (often referred to as the 'Sage of Omaha'), says of cash:

"The one thing I will tell you is the worst investment you can have is cash. Everybody is talking about cash being king and all that sort of thing. Cash is going to become worthless over time. But good businesses are going to become worth more over time."[6]

If you want to grow your money, you are going to need to take on some risk – i.e., the chance that you will lose some of your money. There is no way of earning more on your money than the interest on cash, without taking on some risk. And in general, the more risk you take on, the higher the long-term average return. This is investing – taking on some risk, taking a longer-term view so you can grow your money.

There are two traditional classes of assets used in constructing investment portfolios: equities (also referred to as shares or stocks) and bonds. Equities are ownership shares in a company; bonds are loans to governments and companies. There are other asset classes such as property, commodities (e.g., gold, silver, oil), alternatives (more esoteric investments such as 'hedge funds' and 'private equity'), but for the purposes of this discussion on risk, I will just refer to equities and bonds, as most portfolios for personal investors will comprise only a small proportion of these other assets.

Bonds pay guaranteed interest (referred to as a 'coupon') whereas with equities the 'dividend' paid out depends on how well the company has done and the shareholder has full upside and downside risk. In a good year there may be an extra dividend, but in a bad year there will be none. So, portfolios with a higher proportion of equities (vs bonds) will be higher risk. While these higher risk portfolios will grow more over time, they will also have a higher chance of dropping in value and will fall more when markets dip. Technically these ups and downs are referred to as 'volatility'. Higher volatility = higher risk. Because equities are riskier than bonds, investors expect a higher return on their investment. No rational person would invest in a riskier asset if it didn't offer a higher potential return. So, generally, over time the higher the proportion of equities over bonds, the higher the return, but also the higher the volatility.

The total returns from equities come from two sources:

1. Dividends; and
2. Changes in the share price (the share price can go up or down).

A very profitable company that doesn't pay out dividends, but rather reinvests its profits in growth (e.g., by opening new factories or stores, launching new profitable products), will grow in value and its price will go up, so the investor gets a return even if they don't get a dividend.

It is similar for bonds, only the dynamics are different. The returns for bonds are from the coupon (or interest) paid by the bond and the change in price. But the price of a bond changes when investors' perception of the risk of the bond changes (i.e., they think it is more or less likely that the company or government who has issued the bond won't pay back the capital on maturity) or there's a general change in interest rates paid in the market that affects investors' expected returns. So, when the Bank of England reduces the 'base' rate, it affects perceptions of what a fair rate of return is on other bonds, and investors' expectations of return reduce for all bonds. But if you have an existing bond that's paying a fixed coupon, when interest rates in the market go down, the price of the bond goes up. It sounds a bit counter-intuitive. But, if people are having to accept a lower rate of interest today than they were yesterday, they are now willing to pay more for a bond that delivers a fixed payment (coupon) than they were yesterday.

Every year Barclays Investment Bank publishes its *Barclays Equity Gilt Study*. This study has been tracking the returns on cash, gilts (UK government bonds) and equities all the way back to 1899. The Barclays 2019 study showed that £100 invested in cash in 1899 would be worth just over £20,000 by 2019. If invested in gilts, the same £100 would be worth close to £42,000. However, £100 invested in equities in 1899 would be worth around £2.7m. While the data provides compelling evidence of equities' outperformance over 120 years, unfortunately most of us have far shorter investment horizons.

So, if you have a long time, the most suitable investment strategy is to maximise the risk you take on in your portfolios and have a pure equity portfolio. Generally, if you are in your 20s or 30s this is the right answer – if this money is for retirement you have a 30–50 year investment horizon. However, this must be subject to the level of risk you are willing to accept, or your ability to bear the potential costs of losing money on your investments. This is referred to as your risk tolerance. If you have decades before you need the money or retire, this may be more of a psychological barrier. If you need the money for your retirement within a relatively short time, there is the practical question of how much loss you can afford within that time. If you were in your 50s or 60s you would need to sacrifice long-term performance for greater certainty that you are not going to lose a large proportion of your investment in a market reversal.

The classic balanced portfolio is the 60/40 equity/bond portfolio. This basic construction is the most popular portfolio for advised private clients. This is not surprising. Most private wealth is in the hands of older investors (most of us aren't born with money, we have to make it and that takes time) and the 60/40 portfolio is considered well suited to those nearer retirement. It has provided a good trade-off of good growth while smoothing out the extreme highs and lows (volatility) of a more equity-rich portfolio. But it is not the right portfolio for everyone.

PIMFA (The Personal Investment Management and Financial Advice Association, the trade association for firms that provide investment management and financial advice) identifies five reference portfolios, with the most conservative having just 22.5% equities and the most aggressive being 95% equities.

Another framework for assessing asset allocation impact on risk is that provided by ARC Research (a firm providing investment consulting, manager research and performance reporting services to the wealth and asset management industry). Its Private Client Indices compile data from more than 130,000 professionally managed portfolios. ARC pulls together quarterly reports of the actual performance of these portfolios and produces statistical insights into their performance across the following categories:

- Cautious: below 40% equities
- Balanced: 40% to 60% equities
- Steady growth: 60% to 80% equities
- Equity risk: above 80% equities

Unsurprisingly, most financial advisors and fund managers have four or five 'risk-profiled' offerings in their portfolio ranges.

Financial advisors will typically assess your risk tolerance on a four- or five-point scale (to match the portfolio profiles). There are a number of simple tests online that you can use to test your risk tolerance (more about this in Chapter 6). Financial advisors have a regulatory obligation to ensure that the investors are put into investments that are 'suitable', and they do this by assessing their client's risk appetite and then investing them in portfolios that match that appetite. From looking at publicly available data for investment funds we know that the most investments are in medium- or medium- to high-risk funds. Matching these to the PIMFA portfolios would have portfolios with 62.5% equities (profile 3) to 77.5% equities (profile 4). As noted before, older people tend to have more money, so these profiles reflect the risk tolerances of older investors. If you are early in your investment journey with many decades before you need to draw on your investment, then you should be in the 100% equity profile.

As an investor you need to have a clear understanding of the risks of investing in the markets. In particular you need to know how much the markets can go down in value in any one episode (referred to as 'drawdowns') and how long markets typically take to recover from these events. This knowledge will help you stay the course when the inevitable market dips come along, and stop you cashing in your investment when the turbulence hits. Fortunately, the significant drawdowns of the past 20 years have recovered quickly. It took about 4 years for the market to recover past their pre-crisis peak for the 2007/8 Great Recession and a similar length of time to recover from the early 2000s 'dot.com' crash. The Covid-19 crash of early 2020 was even shorter, with most markets recovering to their pre-crash levels in less than a year. However, recoveries have not always been that quick. The markets took about 25 years to recover to their pre-crisis peak after the Great Depression of 1929. The peak to trough drawdown was around 50% for the 2007/8 Great Recession and around 33% for the early 2000s recession, but close to 90% for the Great Depression of 1929.

We have to hope that we will never see a drawdown as deep or as long as the Great Depression again. Of course, in that case the markets also had to contend with the protracted and costly World War II. And governments and central banks are much more active these days in their response to market events and see it as essential to take quite aggressive measures to maintain market stability. However, investors in an equity-only portfolio need to at least be prepared for losses of the scale of the major drawdowns of the past 20 years and the potential of having to wait four years (or quite possibly more) for their portfolios to get back to where they were.

Unfortunately, bond yields are at historic lows, so investing in bonds often means losing out significantly in the long term. The safest bonds (issued by governments) pay out much less than inflation, so like cash, investors in these bonds lose money every day.

There has been quite a bit of speculation as to whether the traditional 60/40 portfolio (and its variants) work in this era of very low bond yields. Post the Great Recession of 2007/8, yields on bonds came right down as central banks around the world lowered base rates to close to zero (to protect their economies) and rates have stayed down. While over the intervening years rates came up a bit, central banks reversed this trend in response to the Covid-19 crisis and rates are again at historic lows.

In an equity/bond portfolio, the bonds act as a counterbalance to the equity risk. The way this works is as the market yield comes down, the price of the bonds usually goes up. This is because bonds offer a coupon fixed at the time of issue – if yields (coupons) come down for new bond issues, those holding existing bonds can sell the bonds for a higher price because investors are willing to pay more for each pound of coupon, given the low yield on new issues. So, the bond counterweight was very effective.

However, if yields are already very low (as they are now), the opportunity for them to go lower is more limited, so the counterweight becomes less effective. Theoretically central banks can reduce rates to negative, and in some countries, this has happened, but most central banks are reluctant to do this. Also, recently we have seen instances where bond and share prices have both fallen at the same time, suggesting to some that the counterweight effect of bonds is on the wane.

However, the consensus amongst investment professionals is that the balanced portfolio of equity and bonds, including the classic 60/40 portfolio, is here to stay. Historically bond prices generally rise when equities fall, even in periods of negative interest rates. While this sometimes breaks down, and the prices of bonds and equities fall (or rise) together, this generally only lasts for a short period of time after which the usual inverse relationship between bonds and equities re-establishes itself.

Not all bonds are the same. Government bonds of developed economies (such as 'US Treasuries' or 'UK Gilts') typically have the lowest yields, as investors are pretty certain they will get their money back at the end of the term. 'Blue chip' bonds (bonds issued by the most stable, well-known companies) will have a higher yield, as there is a higher risk of default. The bonds issued by emerging market governments will pay a higher rate of interest than developed market government bonds and the bonds issued by more risky companies, referred to as 'high-yield' bonds, pay more than those issued by blue chip companies.

When faced with the issues of very low bond yields, most portfolio managers manage this risk by reducing the proportion of low-yielding government bonds and increasing the proportion of higher-yielding bonds (such as corporate or emerging market bonds). Others will increase the ratio of other assets that are in the portfolio, such as real estate. Still others argue that this reduces the case for a bond-heavy portfolio and investors are better off taking on more equity risk.

This needs to be viewed in the light of other trends pushing to more equity-heavy portfolios. Historically, retirement investors had a fixed horizon as most were required to invest the bulk of their pension pot in an annuity on retirement. However, in 2015 the UK government announced a set of 'pension freedoms' and because of this change most retirees keep their portfolio intact post retirement and 'drawdown' a pension in retirement. This increases the risk to the pensioners' income (from investment volatility) but yields on retirement annuities are meagre compared to the expected return on a diversified portfolio. So now retirement investment portfolios are typically invested for a much longer horizon and it can be argued that a lower ratio of bonds in portfolios can be justified.

For younger investors it is anyway best to have your portfolio heavily weighted towards equities. Young investors typically have a long-time horizon to recover from any portfolio drawdown, and so can and should take on more investment risk than older investors. In Chapter 6, we will talk more about how you practically assess your own risk tolerance and identify the profile of portfolio that is right for you.

In summary:

- Cash is not an investment and you should not leave long-term money in cash.
- Generally, the more risk you take on in your portfolio the better the return.
- And portfolios with a higher proportion of equities (shares in companies) vs bonds (loans to companies) will be higher risk but have higher returns.
- If you have enough time (i.e., many decades) the most suitable investment strategy is to maximise your portfolio risk and have a pure equity portfolio.
- But this portfolio will be much more 'volatile', i.e., its value is liable to change quickly and unpredictably.
- And you may not have the 'risk tolerance' for a very volatile portfolio; i.e., you may be unwilling or unable to accept this level of fluctuation in the value of your portfolio.
- You need to assess your risk tolerance (and there are tools to help you do this) to decide how much risk you should take on in your portfolio.
- It is important that you have a clear understanding of the risk of investing in the markets, how much they can reverse (or drawdown) and how long they will take to recover.

2

DIVERSIFICATION

"THE ONLY FREE LUNCH IN FINANCE"

In this chapter I am going to explain what it means to diversify your investments, why this is important and how buying a ready-made fund is the simplest way to invest in a diversified portfolio.

This is one we have probably all heard about before. The expression "*don't put all your eggs in one basket*" is well entrenched. We even teach this to our children. But what does this mean for investments? Of course, it means you shouldn't invest in just one or a few companies, you need a good spread. But it also means you shouldn't just invest in one sector of the equity markets (e.g., all financial services or all manufacturers), or just in a single geography (e.g., the UK) or just in one asset class (e.g., just equities).

Diversification does not eliminate the risk of the value of your portfolio reversing (going down in value), but it will reduce the depth of the reversal, while optimising the upside. For example, if you own shares in 10 companies, in different

stry sectors, and one of the companies lands in difficulty,
e chances are the others will still carry on as before and will
cushion you from the loss on that one share. Similarly, if you
have shares in companies in the UK and say the US, your US
shares will cushion the losses from a UK domestic event, such
as we had with the Brexit vote fallout.

Harry Markowitz, the Nobel laureate pioneer of 'Modern
Portfolio Theory' called diversification *"the only free lunch in
finance"*. Surprisingly, when you blend assets in a portfolio you
don't end up with just the average of the risk and return profiles
of the blended assets; you end up with a better return for any
given level of risk. As you can see on the graph below, a 60/40
portfolio ends up with a performance above what we would
expect from a simple blend of the two assets.

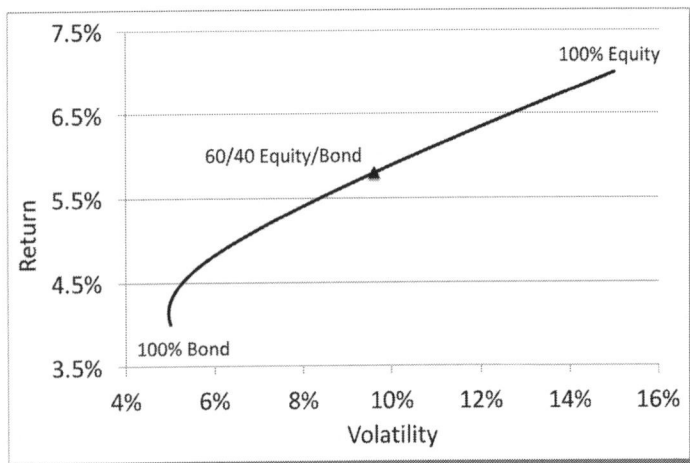

Figure 3: The power of diversification

Why is this? While the expected return of a portfolio is the
weighted average of the returns of the individual components,

the portfolio risk ends up being lower than the weighted average of the risk of its components.

For example, for a 60/40 equity/bond portfolio, where equity returns are 7% and bond returns are 4%, the portfolio expected return would be:

Portfolio expected return = 60/100 x 7% + 40/100 x 4% = 5.8%

However, because the risk/return profile of these components are 'uncorrelated', i.e., they don't all react in the same way to market events, the risk of the combined portfolio is always lower than the simple weighted average. The maths is complicated for volatility, but if you really want to know, read the endnote![7]

Particularly interesting is the small 'hockey stick' kickback at the bond end of the curve. Adding a small amount of equity to a bond portfolio reduces the riskiness (volatility) of the portfolio while increasing expected return. At first this sounds wrong – how can adding something more risky to a low risk portfolio make it even less risky while increasing its return? But of course, these assets are not closely correlated. Or to put it another way, when bond prices are dropping, much of the time equity prices won't be. So, by adding a bit of equity you actually reduce the risk of the overall portfolio. This only works for a small amount of equity; beyond a certain point, the greater volatility of the equity asset dominates the portfolio.

In summary, make sure to have a well-diversified portfolio and enjoy the free lunch!

Diversification won't make you rich. The return you will get is the average across your underlying investments. With perfect foresight, you could concentrate your portfolio in the higher-performing assets. But we know that we can't make the right choices repeatedly and reliably. Diversification provides protection from the downside and provides a smoother return profile, ensuring you have a much better chance of meeting your investment objectives and helping you to sleep better at night.

So how do you do this in practice? The simplest way is to buy a ready-made fund where someone else has worked out the optimum allocation of assets within the portfolio. Most large asset managers have these products on their shelves. Ready-made funds are sometimes also referred to as 'multi-asset' funds. Having read Chapter 1, it will not surprise you to hear that ready-made funds typically come in four or five risk profiles to accommodate the different levels of risk appetite across different investors. They will have labels like, 'cautious' for a fund with a high proportion of bonds vs equity, or 'adventurous' for a fund with a high proportion of equities, and 'balanced' for the classic 60/40 equity/bond fund. You already know that younger investors should put their long-term savings into the most equity-rich versions of these ready-made funds.

Financial advisors invest their client's money using ready-made funds. They don't build tailored investment portfolios for each of their clients. Rather they pick a good portfolio manager, who has done all the hard work of building a set of well-diversified ready-made funds and use one of the four or five risk variants for their client. There is a whole industry built up around the manufacture and distribution of these funds. Most of the large firms have built their own range of ready-made funds (e.g., HSBC and Hargreaves Lansdown). Of course, this also ensures the firm captures some of the funds' revenue and it doesn't all go to third party asset managers. Many of the smaller independent advisors will use the funds of other larger wealth and asset managers for their clients, e.g., from Abrdn or Blackrock.

The decisions regarding the long-term allocation to different asset classes in portfolios are referred to as 'strategic asset allocation' (SAA). To determine the optimal allocation, quantitative analysts use historical data to model an 'efficient frontier' of risk and performance. They will then use this model to inform the SAA for each risk profile of their multi-asset portfolios. As time goes on, each asset class will perform at different levels and the portfolio manager will need to 'rebalance' the portfolio to maintain the SAA. If they don't do this, the portfolio will end up having a higher proportion of the assets that have grown the most and will drift away from the ideal allocation for the targeted risk profile.

Portfolio managers may also make tactical tweaks to the asset allocation to take advantage of short-term opportunities in the relative prices of the asset classes. For example, if they think developed market equities are overpriced, they may sell down a (typically small) proportion of their holdings and increase the amount of cash or of some other asset that they think represents better value in the short term. These short-term tweaks to the asset allocation are referred to as 'tactical asset allocation' (TAA).

Ready-made funds come in different risk profiles, but there are also options you need to consider. Some of the funds will adopt an 'active' investment strategy, while others will take a 'passive' approach. More and more investors are demanding that their investments are responsible and sustainable and that their fund managers include environmental, social and governance (ESG) factors in their portfolio decisions. The next chapter will talk you through these options.

In summary:

- In investing, diversification means having a spread of companies, market sectors, geographies and asset classes in your portfolio.
- Diversification does not eliminate the risk of your portfolio reversing (going down in value), but it will reduce the depth of the reversal, while optimising the portfolio's return.
- A diversified portfolio ends up having a better return for any given level of risk than just the weighted average of the risk/return of each individual component.
- This outperformance effect of diversification was referred to as the "*only free lunch in finance*" by Harry Markowitz, the Nobel Laureate pioneer of modern portfolio theory.
- The simplest way to invest in a well-diversified portfolio is to buy a ready-made fund where someone else has worked out the optimal asset allocation. Younger investors should put their long-term savings into the most equity-rich versions of these ready-made funds.
- A long-term asset allocation view is referred to as the 'Strategic Asset Allocation' (SAA), while 'Tactical Asset Allocation' (TAA) refers to shorter-term views to take advantage of short-term opportunities.

3

PORTFOLIO STRATEGIES

ACTIVE VS PASSIVE, AND ESG

If you have been reading, watching or listening to anything about investing you will have heard about 'active' vs 'passive' investing. You will also have heard about 'sustainable' investing, and/or ESG (Environmental, Social and Corporate Governance) investing. In this chapter I will explain the difference between active and passive funds and why, generally, you should invest in a passive rather than an active fund. I will also explain sustainable or ESG investing, and the different 'flavours' of ESG funds and the choices in ESG investment funds.

ACTIVE VS PASSIVE

There are two broad approaches to investing – active and passive. With an active fund, the portfolio manager selects the individual shares, bonds, etc. that go into the portfolio, picking the ones they believe will outperform the market sector they are investing in. So, an active manager in UK equities will buy shares in those UK companies they believe will perform better than the average UK company. Whereas with a passive fund the portfolio manager just buys all shares in the market sector they are investing in, with the aim of doing no better or worse than the average performance in that sector. Passive investing is often referred to as 'index investing' – as the portfolio manager just buys all the shares in the index that best represents the market sector he or she is investing in, for example, the FTSE 100 index, the index of the 100 largest companies listed on the London stock exchange. Jack Bogle, the founder of the passive fund powerhouse, Vanguard, famously said: "*Don't look for the needle in the haystack. Just buy the haystack.*"

When you buy a passive ready-made fund, you are buying the asset allocation view of the fund manager, so it is not truly passive. However, the manager is not trying to outperform the underlying market in each asset class, they are just buying the overall performance of the market through the index. When you buy an active multi-asset fund, in addition to the asset allocation view, you are also buying their view of how to outperform the market in each underlying sector.

Active investing is a zero-sum game – for every investor that beats the market there must be another investor who lost out. All investors as a group earn the overall return of the market, no more or less. After fees it is actually worse. As Jack Bogle put it, after the deduction of the costs of investing, beating the stock market is a loser's game. Active funds are more expensive than passive funds, with the cheapest passive ready-made fund costing just 0.17% (Blackrock MyMap Fund) of the assets under management (AuM), whereas similar active funds start at around 0.75%. So, the active fund must outperform the equivalent passive fund by at least 0.6% each year to be worth buying. In many cases the costs of active management are much higher, leaving an even greater performance hurdle for the active manager.

While the average active funds don't outperform their passive rivals, of course the better ones do. However, even those that do outperform over the short-term struggle to do so consistently over the medium- to long-term. Over the medium- to long-term the fund manager's performance 'reverts to the mean'. There is good performance initially, but over time the good/lucky picks end up being matched by the bad/unlucky picks and the fund performance eventually ends up as just average. It is a bit like the game of tenpin bowling I played with some of my colleagues a little while ago; my first couple of throws were good with a 'strike' and a 'spare' and I was up at the top end of the leader board for a while, but as the game went on my very average skill became apparent, and I slowly drifted down the rankings. Morningstar (the fund research services firm) publishes a semi-annual Active/Passive Barometer that measures the performance of US active funds against their passive peers. In its December 2019 report it found that while in 2019 almost half (48%) of funds outperformed the average passive (up from 38% in 2018), over the 10 years to end 2019 only 23% of active funds beat their passive rivals.

Therefore, if you are going to invest in active funds you need to pick the long-term winners. Unfortunately, selecting the winning funds in advance is more difficult than it looks. Past performance is not a predictor of future success. Some of the advisory firms and multi-asset managers have teams of highly qualified analysts focused on this full-time and again on average they don't do any better than the market net of fees over the long-term.

Why is this? We know that markets aren't perfectly efficient. So why can't very bright, well-educated fund managers outperform the average investor? The problem is the 'average investor' is now also very bright and well educated. This has changed markedly over the past 50 years. In the 1970s around 90% of the investors trading on US exchanges were individuals who averaged one trade every year or two. Today 98% is done by institutions or algorithmic trading computers who are in the market all day and every day. Rules on public disclosure for listed companies have ensured that everyone trades on the same information, with penalties for trading on inside information; and the flow of information is virtually instantaneous with over 300,000 Bloomberg terminals spewing all sorts of data and analysis 24 hours a day[8]. It is a bit like professional football; it is very difficult to do any better than just draw against the opposing team, because they are all just so good.

It is rough being an active manager. If you are conservative and defensive, and good (or lucky), your performance at best will be just a little bit better than the index and may even be accused of being a 'closet tracker' – charging active fees for passive performance. If you are bold and have strong contrarian views you could do very well for a stretch. But when the market turns against your view, your fund will do very badly, and your investors will flee. For the investor, this also means if you pick a star active manager you have to be prepared for the possibility that your manager's bets could go horribly wrong.

The recent debacle with Neil Woodford's funds is a case in point. In 2014 Woodford and his business partner, Craig Newman, left their long-time employer, Invesco Perpetual, to launch their own fund. In the prior 25 years Woodford had built a stellar track record as the manager of two of Invesco's most popular retail funds totalling over £25bn. Such was his personal following, and his and his partner's ability to persuade key fund distributors to follow him, that they were able to raise over £5bn within months of starting the firm. Over 3 years the fund grew to £15bn (both new investment and growth). However, by the second half of 2017 the performance of the fund started to reverse and while many of his most ardent admirers stuck with him, others began to divest. Eventually the trickle turned to a flood, and when the Kent County Council, one of Woodford's longest-standing clients, decided to recoup its investment of over £250m, there wasn't the cash to pay, and the fund had to be suspended locking in hundreds of thousands of remaining investors indefinitely. At the time of writing this is still unwinding, but it is estimated that investors could lose more than half their money.

It is often argued that active managers can go 'defensive' when markets are inflated or at times of heightened uncertainty. For example, a defensive play could involve buying shares in supermarkets, and selling shares of companies selling luxury products, on the assumption that in a downturn the sales of basic staples hold up better than those of luxury goods. This ability to make defensive trades potentially positions active managers as less risky in downturns. Active funds should theoretically have some advantage when markets are falling. An active manager can take some action while a passive manager has to just stand back and watch. Unfortunately, as we know, it is very difficult to 'time the market' and very few active managers get this right. If they go defensive too early, they could significantly underperform ahead of the peak. Data from the COVID-19 induced market dip is varied at best. Morningstar tracked the performance of a range of indices and found that only 42% of active US stock funds beat their indices in the initial COVID decline (20 February – 16 March, 2020), with the average fund lagging the index by 0.42%.

The trend to passive has gone overwhelmingly mainstream in recent years. In September 2019, Bloomberg reported an end of an era and that US passive equity funds had "*finally eclipsed old-fashioned stock pickers*". After years of gaining ground on actively managed funds the investment industry reached one of the biggest milestones in its modern history as assets in US index-based mutual funds and exchange-traded funds (ETFs) topped those in active stock funds for the first time. While active funds still make up around 70% of invested assets under management in the UK, the flow is strongly towards index funds. In 2020, £35.7bn was added to UK domiciled investment funds, of which £33.1bn went into passive funds[9]. Investors are voting strongly in favour of the index fund, and fewer and fewer are convinced that active management is worth paying for.

ESG (Environmental, Social and Corporate Governance)

A further dimension to consider is ESG or 'responsible investing'. Instead of looking solely at economic factors, more and more investors are looking for their portfolios to reflect the right ethical choices in their selections. They want their funds to include environmental, social and corporate governance factors. The term ESG covers environmental issues like climate change and resource scarcity, social issues like labour practices, product safety and data security and governance matters, like board diversity, executive pay and business ethics.

Historically, there has been an assumption that there was a trade-off and that investors would have to sacrifice performance when investing ethically, but research has shown that this is not necessarily the case. To quote just one example, research conducted for the Credit Suisse Global Investment Returns Yearbook (2020) concluded that over the longer-term, certain types of ESG screening strategies need not compromise risk-adjusted returns. Intuitively it makes sense that companies that are responsible and operate sustainably should be more resilient and perform better over the long-term.

While there has long been a demand for portfolios that sifted out tobacco and/or gambling and/or weapons (so-called 'sin shares'), responsible investing considering broader ESG factors is relatively new. But it is now becoming more mainstream. Approaches to ESG vary. At its most basic, the asset manager uses its 'voice' to engage with companies to improve their ESG practices. 'Exit' is a more activist approach and sees companies being avoided or divested that fail ethical criteria.

The UN is now in on the act, setting up the UNPRI (UN Principles for Responsible Investing), an initiative to encourage better investment practices. Most major fund houses are now signatories to the principles. Though, until now, these requirements are mostly 'voice' and have not been particularly demanding, with some justified criticism of 'greenwashing', they at least ensure ESG gets considered in investment processes. Larry Fink, the CEO of Blackrock (the world's largest fund manager, with $9 trillion in assets), unveiled sweeping changes in January 2020 to focus the firm on sustainable investing. For example, he has pledged to eliminate companies that derive more than a quarter of their revenue from thermal coal from its actively managed portfolios. Given the size of Blackrock, the roll-out of this strategy will have a huge impact.

Generally, the ESG approaches adopted by fund managers can be divided into three categories:

1. Negatively screened;
2. Positively managed; and
3. Impact.

Negatively screened funds avoid investing in companies that are engaged in harmful activities such as tobacco, gambling, thermal coal, oil sands or weapons manufacture. Positively managed funds will seek to include firms leading their sector in terms of ESG credentials. They may also focus the fund on a specific area of activity such as renewable energy or equal opportunities. Impact funds target their investments on firms making a positive impact on environment or society, for example, by investing in firms tackling climate change, pollution or inequality.

Historically, almost by definition, ESG investing needed to be active. So, while investors in an ESG fund did not necessarily have to sacrifice performance, they did end up paying more in fees than the non-ESG passive investor. That is changing, underpinned by the growth in ESG indices and ESG 'Exchange-Traded Funds' (ETFs) that track these indices. In 2009 there were 35 sustainable ETFs and by January 2020 there were over 300[10]. These indices tend to be focused on negative screening approaches. They start with the universe of companies in the specific index, e.g., the 'FTSE 100' index (the index of the 100 largest companies listed on the London Stock Exchange) and then filter out companies that don't pass the screen criteria or an overall constraint. So, as well as screening out tobacco, weapons, thermal coal, etc., they may also target the reduction of the carbon intensity of the overall index by a specific percentage.

One of the challenges with ESG is the lack of consensus as to what constitutes an ESG investment product. Some players have labelled their products as ESG, while still holding problematic assets such as oil, weapons or tobacco, resulting in claims of greenwashing. Work is being done by regulators, industry bodies and the major industry firms to standardise ESG ratings, but until then, investors need to exercise caution and do their own research to verify the position.

My youngest daughter has some money in an investment account. I know she wants to act responsibly in investing this money, so I showed her a fact sheet for a low-cost ESG fund that I thought would be suitable. She had a quick look and then pointed out some of the companies in the top ten holdings, which included Amazon, Facebook, Alphabet (Google's parent) and JPMorgan. In her view, many of these companies are not 'responsible' investments. Of course, this fund is an example of a 'negatively screened' fund, and only screens out exposure to certain types of firms (including tobacco, weapons, thermal coal and oil sands). She is looking for a fund that uses impact investing more actively to have a positive impact on the environment.

The professionals have a similar challenge in reaching consensus as to what constitutes an ESG investment. Take Tesla: clearly, it can lay claim to very strong environmental credentials through its impact on vehicle emissions; however, its governance rating is more problematic. Most notably Tesla's founder and CEO has been rapped on the knuckles by the SEC (the US regulator) over his use of Twitter. As a result, different ratings agencies come to different overall ESG scores for Tesla.

While there is a plethora of ESG funds tracking particular indices, that activity has not yet translated into ready-made passive ESG funds. At the time of writing, there is just one and that's the recently launched Blackrock MyMap 5 Select ESG, which is available in just the one risk flavour, allocating approximately 64% to equity, 33% to bonds and 3% to other assets. So, if you want something more (or less) equity rich you are going to have to look elsewhere for now. One option is to go for a robo-advisor offering, where there are a small number of firms providing a passive portfolio of ESG ETFs. Another is to go for a broad global ESG index fund such as the iShares MSCI World Screened ETF. This isn't strictly a 'ready-made' fund, in that your asset allocation is set by what's in the index and can't be optimised by the fund manager, but it is a broad index, so will give a good diversified exposure. All these options are based on negatively screened indices, so may not suit what you want to achieve with your ESG investing. You may well need to look at an active fund if you want to do more.

The ESG investors' options are continually expanding. Blackrock has promised to double its range of ESG ETFs to 150 by the end of 2021, and, I am told, it will build out its MyMap ESG offering over the next year. Other players in the passive space won't be far behind.

In summary:

Active vs passive
- With an 'active' fund the portfolio manager selects the individual shares that go into the portfolio, picking the ones they believe will outperform their peers.
- With a 'passive' or 'index' fund the portfolio manager aims to replicate the performance of the entire market.
- Active investing is a 'zero-sum' game; for every winner who beats the market, there must be a loser. After fees it is worse, as active funds are more expensive than passive funds.

- If you are going to invest in active funds, you need to be sure of your ability to pick long-term winners. This is very difficult, if not impossible, to do with any certainty of success.
- Passive investing has become more popular in recent years. For the US, as of 2019, assets in passive funds exceeded those in active funds.

ESG

- Including Environmental, Social and Governance (ESG) factors in portfolio management has become more important to investors.
- While there has long been a demand for portfolios that sifted out tobacco and/or gambling and/or weapons, 'responsible investing' considering broader ESG factors is relatively new.
- One of the challenges of ESG investing is the lack of consensus as to what constitutes responsible investing. This is improving as the industry matures.
- Also, the 'passive' ESG offerings are currently limited, and you may need to consider more expensive active funds.

4

TAX-EFFICIENT INVESTING

ISAS AND PENSIONS

The government encourages savings with tax breaks through ISAs ('Individual Savings Accounts') and pensions. Essentially, these are 'wrappers' around your investments that provide tax breaks.

You can invest up to £20,000 a year into an ISA and, for most of us, up to £40,000 a year into a pension. That's £60,000 a year for each individual, and of course as a couple it would be £120,000. Not many people are in a position to invest more than this in a year, so, for most of us, all of our investment funds should be in one or both of these wrappers.

What's the difference between a pension and an ISA? In short, with a pension you save pre-tax but pay (some) tax when you eventually withdraw money from the pension, whereas with an ISA you invest with after-tax money, but when you take it out you don't pay any tax. With both you don't pay any tax on the money while it's inside the ISA or pension wrapper.

So how do these work and how much should you invest in each?

PENSIONS

If you work for a company, it is likely that you will automatically be investing into a pension. There are broadly two types of pension fund: 'defined benefit' and 'defined contribution'. As the names imply, a defined-benefit pension pays a specified amount in retirement and your employer takes on the investment risk, whereas with a defined contribution fund you are regularly contributing to build up an investment pot to draw on in retirement, but you take the investment risk. If you work for the public sector, the chances are you are in a defined benefit plan with a guaranteed income in retirement as a function of your years of service. If you work for anyone else, it's likely you are in a defined contribution plan.

'Auto-enrolment' was first introduced in 2008, and now the law requires that most employees be automatically enrolled in a pension scheme unless the employee opts out. Under this scheme your employer deducts a minimum of 5% from your salary each month and provides a further 3% matching contribution, investing this total of 8% into a pension. It's planned that this percentage will go up further in the future. If you work for a larger and/or more benevolent company it may well be that their matching is even more generous than 3%, and if they are even more generous than that they will match some of your additional voluntary pension contributions. In all cases the best course of action is simple: make sure you contribute at least as much as you need to, so you get the full available matching from your firm. This is free money so don't leave it on the table!

Beyond this minimum, how much should go into a pension vs ISA? Pensions are very tax efficient overall, more so than

ISAs, so you want to maximise the benefit of this tax saving. But you can only take money out of a pension when you are older, usually somewhere between age 55 and 65, whereas you can withdraw your money at any time from an ISA. Also, pensions are a bit complicated and you can end up paying punitive tax if you over-contribute, so you do need to work through this carefully. For younger investors the right answer is usually to pay just enough into your pension to ensure you get all your employer matching, but no more, and put any other savings into an ISA.

To explain:

A pension's tax efficiency comes from two sources:

1. The difference in your tax rate when you pay in and the tax rate when you eventually take your pension.
2. The tax-free 25% you get when you take your pension.

To explain (1) above by an example: If you pay into your pension when you are earning say £60,000 a year, your top tax rate will be 40% and so every extra pound that you put into a pension will only cost you 60p in take-home pay[11]. When you retire, you generally have, and need, less income (the house is paid for/kids off your hands/no commuting etc) so, say you draw a pension of £30,000, your top tax rate will be only 20%. So you end up taking money out of the pension at a lower rate of tax than you saved when you put it in. In this case, each pound you put in cost you 60p, but after tax you get 80p when you take it out. Arguably, if your top rate of tax is 20%, you don't get this tax benefit, unless you plan on a pension that's at the zero rate of tax (less than £12,570 a year), but I would not recommend that!

The tax-free 25% is available to everyone. When you start drawing on your pension you are able to take 25% as a tax-free lump sum or you can take the first 25% of every withdrawal or payment tax-free as you go. So, at worst, you save 25% tax over your lifetime for any money saved into a pension, but you could save even more from the difference in your tax rates while working vs retired.

But there is a complication, and that is that you can 'overfund' a pension and end up paying punitive tax. There are two numbers you need to understand to make sure you don't overfund (1) the Annual Allowance and (2) the Lifetime Allowance. The annual allowance is the amount you can save each year without paying punitive tax. For most it's £40,000 a year (generally, if you earn more than £240,000 in a year, it starts tapering down until if you earn £312,000, it's only £4,000 a year). If you contribute more than this in any one year you will pay tax on the excess amount you put into your pension and you'll still have to pay tax when you take it out on retirement, so you don't want to do this! But, of course, the Annual Allowance is only really a worry for the very wealthy few who have that sort of income. However, the Lifetime Allowance is one for most of us to watch. It is currently £1,073,000, and it is the most you are allowed to have in your pension pot before you pay a punitive tax. It sounds like a lot, but over 30-40 years of dedicated savings it's quite possible to exceed this amount, especially if the allowance doesn't get increased in line with inflation. It used to be increased by inflation each year, but in early 2021 the government announced that it would freeze all increases until the 2025/26 tax year. Perversely, this is not measured on what you put in, but rather what your pot is worth when you first withdraw from it, so if you have a few good years in investment performance and go over this amount, the taxman will take his slice!

So, for most people under 30, it probably makes sense to just invest in your pension up to the point where you get the maximum from employer matching, but no more, and then invest the rest into an ISA. If you are over 30, it's worth starting to take a view of how you will use this allowance over the next 30 or so years. Clearly, if you are a higher-rate taxpayer this is worth more to you than if you are a basic-rate taxpayer, so if you project you will be a higher-rate taxpayer during that time, you will want to plan to ramp up your pension contributions when you start paying the higher rate. (And if you think your income will eventually reach the levels where the annual allowance tapers off, you will want to maximise your contribution in the years when you put in up to £40,000 so you don't end up not being able to use much of your Lifetime Allowance once your income starts limiting your contributions.)

If you are self-employed and don't have a company pension, you should still invest some of your savings in a pension. The tax advantage is worth having. Most platforms and robo-advisors have a pension offering. Mostly these are SIPPs (Self-Invested Personal Pensions) where you can choose your own underlying investments.

One last thing before we leave the topic of pensions. If you are in a DC company pension scheme, check how your money is invested. Virtually all DC schemes will give you a choice of investments, but if you don't take up the choice, they will put you in the default fund, and the chances are that default fund will be a balanced (60/40) expensive active fund. If you are young, you want to select the 100%-equity low-cost passive option. It may take a bit of work, they don't always make this easy to do, but you should do this. Your accumulated company pensions could well become one of your major assets in time, but that won't be the case if it's all invested in low-growth high-cost funds.

ISAs

With ISAs there are just the two varieties (for adults[12]) to consider, the regular ISA or the Lifetime ISA (LISA). The LISA is only available to you if you are under 40 when you first open it, and normally you can only withdraw without penalty to buy your first home (and only if that home costs less than £450,000) or once you are over 60. The big advantage of a LISA is the government gives you 25% of what you contribute, up to the allowed maximum contribution of £4,000 every year up to age 50. So, if you put in the full £4000, the government will give you another £1000 straight away, making a total of £5000 a year of investment. That's a 25% return right away, so if you can afford to do this, it's a no-brainer, but you need to be sure you are not going to need to take this out before you buy that house or until you are 60. If you withdraw otherwise, you lose 25% of what you withdraw, i.e., all the government bonuses plus, in effect, a 6.25% penalty. My theory is this penalty was not intentional, but that whoever it was who was tasked with writing the formula in the regulations on the day was an arts graduate, whose grasp of basic arithmetic was weak.; $1 + 25\% = 1.25$, but $1.25 - 25\% = 0.9375$. But perhaps I am being unfair. The government suspended this penalty during the pandemic (up until 5 April 2021), to assist those who need emergency access to long-term savings but declined to extend it, on the basis this is intended to be a long-term savings plan and withdrawal should be discouraged. No doubt the fact that this is a very generous/expensive offer from the government was a factor in this decision; the government saves a lot of money from the returned bonuses when people cash in their LISAs.

If you are saving more than £4000 into an ISA or are over 40 and don't already have a LISA, you need to use a regular ISA.

You can save up to £20,000 a year into ISAs; if you have a LISA and a regular ISA that's £4000 in the LISA and a further £16,000 into a regular ISA.

An investment via an ISA (a regular ISA or a LISA) is made with after-tax money, but once inside the ISA wrapper, there are no taxes on capital gains or income. Also, there is no tax on withdrawing funds from an ISA. There is an opportunity for pensioners to take advantage of this to keep their tax rate low, by blending the drawdown of income across their ISAs and their pension.

In summary:

Pensions
- There are two types of pension fund:
  1. A 'defined benefit' (DB) pension which pays a specified amount in retirement and your employer takes on the investment risk.
  2. A 'defined contribution' (DC) pension where you contribute to building up an investment fund to draw on in retirement, but you take the investment risk.
- Under auto-enrolment most employees are automatically enrolled in a pension.
- You should ensure you save at least enough into any company pension to get the maximum employer-matching contribution.
- And if you are in a DC company pension and are young make sure your money isn't invested in the 'balanced' default fund, but in a 100%-equity low-cost passive fund.
- Pensions are very tax efficient – the money you save is

'pre-tax' and on withdrawal the first 25% is tax-free, the rest is taxed at your tax rate at that time (which may well be lower).

- However, currently you have to wait until 55 before you can withdraw money from your pension and there are risks that you can 'overfund' a pension and pay a punitive tax.

ISAs

- ISA contributions are 'after-tax', but once money is in an ISA, no tax is paid on income/gains or when you withdraw.
- There are two varieties of (adult) ISAs, the Lifetime ISA (LISA) and the regular ISA.
- With the LISA, you have to be under 40 to open it, you can only save £4,000 into it each year and you can only withdraw to buy a house (of less than £450,000), or when you are 60.
- However, in a LISA the government generously contributes a 25% matching bonus each year (up to £1,000).
- With a regular ISA you can save up to £20,000 a year (less anything you have contributed to LISA if you have one).

5

FINANCIAL ADVICE

IN PERSON AND ROBO

When it comes to advice you have two choices: a real person or a 'robo-advisor', where an app leads you through the key service steps. There are limits to what a robo-advisor can do, but where your requirements are straightforward, they can provide a valuable service. For many people, the key advantage of a real person advisor goes beyond the technical advice – it's the support they provide helping their clients stick with the plan. But you don't need an advisor to be a successful investor. This chapter will help you understand what in-person and robo-advisors do, where they are useful and how to choose one if you need one.

IN-PERSON FINANCIAL ADVICE

The names are confusing – Independent Financial Advisor (IFA), Financial Planner, Investment Advisor, Wealth Manager, etc. Some clarification: when used correctly, the term Independent Financial Advisor (IFA) means an advisor who is not restricted by the type of advice they give you, and specifically not restricted as to the providers they can recommend. Most advisors tied to large firms with their own products, such as banks and asset managers, are not independent: they will only sell you products from their own firm. While it might look like an independent advisor is a better idea, in reality, no one advisor can search the full market every time and practically this independence won't make much difference to the value of the offering. However, if you do choose a restricted advisor, you need to first be sure you are happy to be restricted by their firm's offering and that you are convinced of the quality of the products on their panel. Also, their products may be more expensive and the firm may well be making a healthy profit on the product on top of their advice fee.

Firms giving investment advice need to be regulated and the individuals working in those firms who provide the advice to clients need to be professionally qualified. The term 'advice' means a personal recommendation as to what you should do. It needs to be based on an understanding of your particular circumstances and financial objectives. 'Guidance' is broader and includes more general information about financial products and can help you understand the different options before deciding what to do. Any organisation can offer guidance, and they don't need to be a regulated firm. Public bodies such as the Money and Pensions Service offer guidance. These public bodies do not sell financial products, nor do they give advice, but they provide general free and impartial financial information.

Not too long ago, financial advisors were paid a commission on sales of investment products by the product manufacturer or fund manager. This created the wrong incentives and the

UK regulators clamped down on this with the introduction of the 'Retail Distribution Review' (RDR) in 2012. The RDR also required advisors to be clear and transparent up front on costs and charges for advice. At the same time, minimum qualifications for advisors were set down. Advisors now have obligations to their clients, to ensure their recommendations are in their clients' best interest.

Before these regulations came into force, many retail clients thought they were getting 'free' advice or were hazy about the scale of commissions paid to their advisors. Also, there was a strong incentive for advisors to churn clients into new products that added little or no value over their existing investments.

Now most advisors charge their fee as a percentage of assets managed (e.g., 1% of the sum invested), though a few will charge by the hour or a fixed fee for a specific service. While the worst of the misalignment of incentives is gone, there is still a 'bias to action' in the percentage of assets charging model. If an advisor who makes money on a percentage of assets managed advises you to do nothing (i.e., leave your investments where they are), he or she will make no money on that advice. For example, if you are consolidating your pensions from multiple past employer pension plans into a single plan, often the best option is to consolidate them to your current employer's plan, as the ongoing changes will likely be lower than a commercial 'Self-Invested Pension Plan (SIPP)'. But an advisor who lives off the ongoing charges isn't going to make any money if he or she recommends that option.

Even the FCA (the government's Financial Conduct Authority) is a bit uncomfortable with the current charging approach. In a recent policy paper, it said this: "*Ongoing advice charges create a conflict of interest, as an adviser may have a strong monetary incentive to recommend one course of action over another. Over time, these charges can have a significant negative financial impact on the consumer's transferred funds."* and: *"Our view is that many consumers would not benefit from ongoing advice as their circumstances are unlikely to change significantly from year to year[13]."*

You need to be aware that in many cases the model is set up so the advisor is the sales function of the firm. Wealth and asset management firms measure commercial success in terms of investment assets gathered. Their valuations are a function of the annual fee that these assets generate. These firms are valuable to their owners because once the client brings their assets to the firm, providing they do a reasonably good job, the assets will stay for a long time. This is all good for these businesses, but as a potential client you need to understand this, so you can look after yourself and make sure the arrangement works for you as well.

If you are going to employ an advisor, look closely at the charges and preferably don't pay ongoing charges, but rather pay on an hourly or fixed-fee basis for the service you receive at the time. It's likely it will be cheaper in the long run and you will ensure they are not incentivised to make changes unnecessarily. After all that's how you would pay for any other professional service like a lawyer or accountant.

As you will know from reading through the rest of this book, you don't need to pay for an advisor to be a successful investor. However, there is one transaction for which you have to take advice and that is for a transfer from a defined benefit (DB) to a defined contribution (DC) pension. This is a regulatory requirement. This is a good thing as mostly it isn't a good idea to give up the guaranteed retirement income offered by a DB scheme for the market uncertainties of a DC scheme. The regulators are well aware of the complexities of this decision and the risks to consumers from promoters of these transfers, so they made it compulsory to get advice for this. And the IFAs who give this advice are amongst the most qualified, requiring a 'level 6' qualification, vs the 'level 4' minimum qualification required for IFAs.

The capital payouts for giving up on a DB pension are often quite high. This is because these pension funds have to invest in very low-yielding bonds to be able to underwrite the guarantees on these pensions, so they are prepared to pay a high premium to rid themselves of this obligation. If this is a company pension, ultimately the company has to provide support when there is shortfall, so companies are keen to be rid of this risk as well. As a beneficiary of such a fund, you need to think very carefully about giving up on this guarantee. Of course you may get a better return if you invest these funds in a well-diversified balanced fund, but there is no guarantee. If you have a proportion of your pension assets in a DB fund, it may well give you the freedom to take more equity risk in your other investments and 'leverage' up your overall return this way.

There are other reasons to call in the help of a financial advisor from time to time. An advisor can provide a professional, experienced and independent review of your financial plans. You may be too optimistic or pessimistic and a good advisor will help hone and build confidence in your plans. It may be you want to invest into more specialist investments such as a Venture Capital Trust or an Enterprise Investment Scheme, and a specialist advisor can help you navigate the options and build a balanced portfolio. Advisors are trained in personal tax and understand the details of how the pension tax allowances work.

If you are at risk of overfunding your pension or have other complexities, this advice could well save you a lot of money. In addition, their advice can be very valuable in understanding inheritance tax consequences of your plans. They can also advise on life assurance and income protection and make sure you have made adequate plans to insure for the unexpected.

It may be that you need very specific and detailed tax or legal advice, in which case it may be necessary to have a lawyer or a tax accountant advise you. For example, if you or your spouse is 'UK non-domiciled' or a 'US person'[14] you need to be sure you understand the consequences and requirements. One thing that people don't commonly understand is that while generally the full estate passes free of inheritance tax between married partners, this is not the case where one partner is not 'UK domiciled'. If you are in this situation you need to get proper advice to make sure your financial plans are correctly structured and that the provisions for your family are not undercut by an unexpected tax. 'US persons' are required to pay US taxes even if they don't live in the US. In 2015 it was reported in the media that Boris Johnson had settled a US tax bill that he had previously described as 'absolutely outrageous'.[15] Boris, who was born in the US, but hadn't lived there since being a child, ended up being charged US tax on the capital gain on selling his home in north London.

The rules for finding a financial advisor are much like the rules for finding any other professional such as a lawyer or an accountant or even finding a contractor to do work on your home. Ask around and get recommendations from people you know and trust on who they use. Make sure they understand that you are looking for someone who can help on a one-off basis and you don't need ongoing advice. Some firms won't provide services on a one-off basis. If your personal contacts don't yield any good answers, use one of the online listings such as the 'findanadviser' service of the Personal Finance Society (thepfs.org), the trade body for financial advisors, or unbiased.co.uk, a commercial listing service. And then make sure you do your due diligence before you start using their services.

This due diligence should at a minimum include:

- A full understanding of their fee and that it's one-off and not going to be recovered on an ongoing basis in any way.
- A clear understanding both ways of the service you need, and who you will be dealing with at the firm.
- A review of the professional qualifications they hold, and confirmation from the FCA website that they and their firm are authorised to give advice and are in good standing with the FCA.
- If you need specialist tax or legal advice or services linked to their advice, an understanding of how this will be engaged.
- How the advice engagement will work; in terms of how they will work with you, input required from you, time in meetings and documentary output.
- Check on fit – are you the type of customer they are set up to serve (do they want to provide the service you are asking for)?

The quality of financial advisors is variable. There are very good advisors out there, but there are also some quite weak ones. Many advisors come from more of a marketing and sales background, and have had to learn to become advisors, because that's what the regulator now expects and requires. It was only in

2013 that the current minimum qualifications were mandated. So, you need to shop around and do your diligence to make sure you get an adviser whose advice is worth paying for.

ROBO ADVICE

A robo-advisor provides financial advice or investment management advice online. The advice is based on a digital algorithm or decision tree. While sometimes robo-advisors will have real humans providing support to help customers use the platform, generally the advice is provided end to end by the digital platform.

Robo-advisors are cheaper than personal (face to face or telephone) advice services. Typically, there are no upfront costs and an ongoing total fee of 1% of assets (including the costs of the underlying investments), vs 3% or more for human-led advice up front and 2.5% or more ongoing. Essentially most robo-advisors take you through 5 steps: (1) they lead you through a simple questionnaire to assess your risk tolerance; (2) they test your financial goals and model what you need to save to achieve these goals; (3) they walk you through the steps so you can make the decision to invest in an ISA and/or a pension or in a general account outside of these wrappers; (4) they will put together a plan for you to invest in a well-diversified multi-asset portfolio appropriate to your risk tolerance and make it really simple for you to invest in that portfolio; (5) and once you have invested they will provide you with regular updates on your portfolio and other content to help you stay invested through the ups and downs (support your 'composure').

Typically, robo-advisors are strong on ensuring you know how much you need to invest to meet your goal and have the right portfolio for your risk tolerance, but they are limited in what they can do in advising you on how much of that investment should be in each of pensions vs ISAs or elsewhere. The number of variables that need to be taken into account in advising on pension investments is just too many for the form filling on an online portal to be tolerable for the average potential client. Most of us are more tolerant of long tedious questionnaires when there is a real person next to us actually filling out the form. And for pensions there is also the challenge of working out the client's existing arrangements. If someone has a good workplace pension with generous ongoing contributions, the robo needs to know this; if it doesn't it can well result in an overfunded pension with excess tax to be paid.

Robo-advisors typically use passive portfolios. They are cheaper and a lot of the robo's appeal is about being lower cost than human-led advice. Most of them use ETFs (Exchange-Traded Funds – easily tradable tracker funds) as the building blocks and you can easily see a breakdown of the assets in your portfolio.

So, should you use one? Of course, you can do this all more cheaply yourself – a robo will charge around 1% for something you could do for around 0.5%. But for many starting out, investing the extra 0.5% may be worth paying. Say you have a £4,000 LISA, 0.5% is only £20 a year, which is not much extra to pay for the guidance and support that a robo offers. Once your portfolio has grown larger and the absolute extra costs of a robo have grown, you may well decide to take off the training wheels and go full DIY.

In summary:

In-person advice
- Firms giving financial advice need to be regulated and the individuals working in those firms need to be professionally qualified.

- The term 'advice' means a personal recommendation as to what you should do.
- Financial advisors are required to be clear and transparent up front on their costs and charges for advice.
- Most charge their fee as a percentage of assets managed; and some will charge a fixed fee or charge by the hour for their services.
- There is potential 'bias to action' in the percentage of assets charging model, in that it could lead to advice to make changes where doing nothing would be the best option.
- You don't need to take personal financial advice to be a successful investor.
- However, you are required to take advice to transfer from a defined benefit (DB) to a defined contribution (DC) pension given the risks of giving up the guarantees of a DB scheme.
- Also, there are other instances where it is valuable to call on the help of a financial advisor; to provide an independent review of your plans or to advise on specific complex issues.
- The quality of financial advisors is variable and you need to shop around and do your due diligence to make sure you get an advisor whose advice is worth paying for.

Robo-advice
- A robo-advisor provides financial and/or investment management advice on a digital platform.
- Robo-advice is cheaper than in-person advice; typically, around 1% or less of AuM.

- They are generally stronger on 'investment advice' and on how much you should invest and assessing your risk tolerance, but
- They are more limited in financial planning advice and on how much to invest in a pension vs an ISA etc, given the extent of the insight required for this type of advice.
- A robo-advisor could be a very useful starting point for the inexperienced investor, with the extra cost often worth paying in the early years of building a portfolio.

6

ASSESSING YOUR OWN RISK TOLERANCE

HOW MUCH RISK SHOULD I TAKE ON?

Your risk tolerance is the level of risk that you are comfortable taking. It comprises two components – a subjective willingness to take risk and an objective ability to take risk. Some people like the adrenaline that comes from taking risks, others don't and are more risk averse. Most rational people would prefer to take less risk with their investments, but know that without taking on some risk, they won't get a decent return. Younger investors may be able to afford to take on more risk, in that they don't need the money for some time. They have a long investment horizon and have time for the markets to recover. But subjectively they may not be willing to do so. When they see their portfolio losing money in a downswing it may make them anxious and cause them sleepless nights. Investors closer to retirement or in retirement may have an absolute objective limit on how much they can afford to lose without a material impact on their lifestyle. If they take a big loss on their portfolio, they don't have time to recover and it may well impact their standard of living.

One of the key tasks in the advice process is the assessment of a client's risk tolerance. Professional financial advisors will typically use a risk tolerance questionnaire and then combine this with a discussion with the client, to bring into consideration other factors, in assessing a client's risk profile. A questionnaire alone will not produce an accurate outcome unless the client has a good understanding of the risk and rewards of making investments.

With risk tolerance assessments, the education provided in the journey to the assessment is often more useful than the result itself. If you have a full understanding up front of the risk you are taking on in making an investment, you will more likely be able to hold the course and hang in there when the market dips. Put another way, working out your risk tolerance for yourself is going to help build your 'composure' so you stick with the plan and don't bail out of your portfolio as soon as you hit the first market dip. Having a realistic understanding of how much your portfolio might actually go down in value, and how long it will likely take to recover to its former highs, will help you resist the temptation to sell as soon as the markets turn against you.

As a DIY investor, you can access a free risk tolerance questionnaire online, though generally these are offered as teasers by firms that want to offer you further personal or robo-advice. But there is nothing stopping you using these as a reference. Standard Life (a major UK pensions and investment company) has a questionnaire on its website[16]. This simple questionnaire has been built by Oxford Analytics, a provider of risk analytics services to a number of the UK financial advisors.

Most of the robo-advisors will take you through a risk tolerance questionnaire and let you see the result, without you having to commit to investing. Of course, they get your details and the chance to try and sell you their service, so are happy to do this. You can also purchase a risk tolerance questionnaire online. Finametrica, one of the leading providers of risk tolerance tools to the wealth industry (and a subsidiary of Morningstar, the investment management services firm) allows individuals to buy a single risk profile you complete online for a £30 charge. Find them at https://riskprofiling.com/Get-Started/myrisktolerance. It could well be a good investment in your learning about your investing self.

The purpose of determining your risk tolerance is to work out a suitable asset allocation for your portfolio. A more equity-rich portfolio will almost certainly have higher returns (over time), but it will be more volatile than a bond portfolio.

One way to think about your risk tolerance and appropriate asset allocations is based on age and stage of life.

Morningstar ran a set of articles a few years back outlining the following life stage profiles[17]:

- 'Young, free and single', in your early 20s you may want a 90% equity/10% fixed income mix.
- 'Making commitments', in your 30s you could opt for 85% equity/15% fixed income.
- 'Young families', assuming you're 35–50 years of age in this bracket you might have at least 75% in equity and up to 25% in a mix of direct property funds or fixed-income funds.
- 'Making choices', for those of 50–65 years your allocation of assets to equities could reduce to around 60% and the property/fixed-income portion rise to 40%.

- 'In retirement', after around 65 (or when you choose to retire) you're looking at somewhere closer to 50% in fixed income, 40% in equity and 10% in cash.

While it's a bit of a rough cut, it's a useful way to think about your risk tolerance and reinforces the point that the younger you are, the more risk you can afford to take on.

Another way of thinking about this is that young people have more 'human capital' than financial capital (unless they are lucky enough to have a very large inheritance or have sold their start-up for a fortune). The total value of their future earnings is many times the value of any saving and investments. Their future earnings are like a bond whose coupon escalates with inflation. In considering their asset allocation, it can be said that the young already have a massive bond-like asset and can afford to put most or all of their remaining allocation into equities.

Practically speaking, there are two reasons younger investors can and should take on more risk in their portfolios. Firstly, on the basis that eventually the markets always recover from any fall in value and go up: if your investing horizon is measured in many decades, the ups and downs don't actually matter to you. Secondly, should it turn out that this time is different and you do suffer a permanent loss, you have decades to recover from the event through earning and savings.

William Bernstein, in his book *The Intelligent Asset Allocator*, suggests an approach that reminds us that we need to have the stomach for losses if we are going to invest in the markets.

I can tolerate losing [x] % of my portfolio in the course of earning higher returns	Suggested % of portfolio invested in shares
35%	80%
25%	60%
15%	40%
5%	20%
0%	10%

Table 1: Portfolio loss tolerance

This very clearly highlights the risk you need to take on in investing in an equity-rich portfolio. As we saw earlier, the peak to trough drawdown for 100% equities was around 50% for the 2007/8 Great Recession and around 33% for the early 2000s recession and in both cases it took around four years for the market to recover to the pre-crash peak. You need to decide up front that you are willing to take on and live with the level of risk you have chosen, so when the markets reverse you have already made the decision that you are prepared to suffer a loss in your portfolio value along the journey and are able to stay the course.

He also suggests that your maximum equity allocation should be 10 times the number of years until you will have to spend the money. For example, if you need the money in two years' time, your equity allocation should not exceed 20%; if it's 7 years' time, it should not exceed 70%.

You may have more than one objective for your investments with different horizons and so may have different risk tolerances for these investment pots with different objectives.

For example, you may be saving for a deposit on a house and expect to buy a property in 5–7 years' time, but also have some retirement savings that you won't be drawing on for at least 30 years. So, you may consider 80–100% equity appropriate for your pension, but a lower weighting for your house deposit investment plan. Some suggest that even investors in, or close to, retirement should divide their pot into two; with one lower-risk portfolio focused on essential spend, and the other more adventurous portfolio on luxuries like overseas holidays, and if there is anything left over, a legacy. This way they can reduce their stress in knowing the essentials are covered year in and out. And in the good years when their more volatile 'luxuries' portfolio is up, they can splash out and in the down years, they can tighten their belts.

Finally, you could take some guidance from how a 'life cycle' fund adjusts asset allocation over time. A life cycle fund, also sometimes referred to as a 'target date' fund, is a fund in

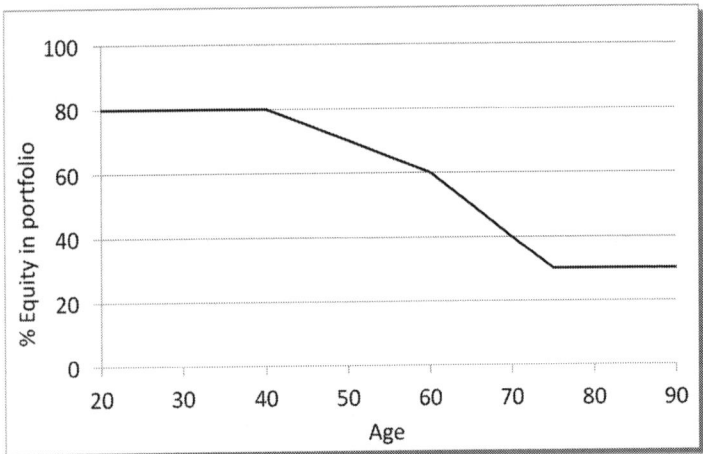

Figure 4: Target date fund glide path

which the asset allocation is automatically adjusted along a 'glide path' to match an investor's risk tolerance as he or she nears retirement. For example, for someone with a target retirement date of 65, the target date retirement funds invest in 80% equities up to age 40, then gradually 'glide' down to 60% equities by age 60 and, then further down to 50% at age 65 and then glide down to 30% equities by age 75, after which they stay at 30% equities.

Ultimately, you need to be able to live with the level of risk you are taking on. You can't be constantly worrying about your portfolio. Until you actually need to use the money and sell out, the ups and downs are just 'paper' gains and losses. Practically it's helpful to build up your investment portfolio over time. In the early years, market swings will cost you £100s and then £1,000s, so that by the time you are losing £10,000s, or even £100,000s, you have got used to it and have gained the composure you need to not let it stress you.

Advisors say clients are generally risk-averse and initially want to take on less risk than they should. They need to be taken on a journey to have it explained that if they want their assets to grow they need to take on risk. Yes, many investors in or near retirement can't afford to take losses and it is right that they limit their downside to some extent. But arguably many younger investors can't afford not to take on risk. If they don't take on risk now, they will never achieve their investment goals.

In summary:
- Your risk tolerance is a measure of your willingness and ability to take on risk.
- The journey of discovery in reaching an assessment

of your risk is often more useful than the assessment result itself. A good understanding of the risk you have taken on will help you better weather the market's up and downs.

- The purpose of determining your risk tolerance is to help you work out a suitable asset allocation for your portfolio.
- The higher the equity content of your portfolio, the greater the tolerance for risk you need to have.
- In general, younger people can and should take on more risk, as they have a longer time to recover from a portfolio reversal.

7

CHOOSING YOUR READY-MADE INVESTMENT

FUNDS OR ROBO-PORTFOLIOS

The cheapest way to set up your ready-made investment is to choose a low-cost ready-made fund and buy it via one of the investment platforms, such as AJ Bell or Hargreaves Lansdown. However, you could also use a robo-advisor, where you get a little more help in assessing which investment is right for you. Also, as I mentioned in the ESG section in Chapter 3, there are not that many options for ESG ready-made funds, so you may decide to go with a robo-advisor because of their ESG offering. Before I take you through the options, I will explain a bit about fund structures.

FUNDS EXPLAINED

An investment fund (or 'mutual fund') is a pool of capital belonging to a number of investors collectively. The fund manager oversees the fund and buys and sells securities (shares, bonds, etc) in line with the fund's investment strategy and scope.

When compared to the alternative of each investor having their own investment account and buying and selling securities in that account, a fund is a much more efficient vehicle. By pooling the assets of multiple investors, it is easier to implement a more diversified portfolio and transaction costs are shared. An individual investor will be limited in the number of shares he can buy. A single (Class A) share in Warren Buffet's Berkshire Hathaway (the most expensive share in the world) costs over $400,000, so most individual investors won't even be able to buy one, let alone include this share in a well-diversified portfolio[18]!

It is also normally more tax efficient as trades within the fund wrapper are not subject to capital gains tax, so the manager can buy and sell underlying securities without any tax constraints or costs. As long as the fund investor continues to hold the fund, no tax will be due on gains, and he or she only pays tax on any gain when the fund is sold (unless of course it's in an ISA or a pension, in which case there is no capital gains tax anyway).

EXCHANGE-TRADED FUNDS (ETFs)

ETFs are a relatively recent innovation with the first ETF issued in 1993. They were initially developed as a way to provide access to market indices for individual investors. For example, there are ETFs that track the FTSE100, the index of the largest 100 companies listed on the London Stock Exchange. Another popular index is the S&P 500, which covers the 500 largest companies traded on US stock exchanges. Given that ETFs are 'exchange traded', there is pricing throughout the day, so an investor can trade in and out of the fund with full knowledge of what price they are getting, whereas traditional funds are only priced once a day. Costs are typically very low relative to other funds. ETFs have grown beyond market indices, with many

ETFs now covering 'smart beta' strategies where the ETF tracks a formulaic investment strategy, such as screening for stocks with high-income yields.

FUND OF FUNDS OR MULTI-MANAGER FUNDS

Most ready-made funds are funds of funds, also referred to as multi-manager funds. A passive ready-made fund will typically be a fund of index funds with separate index funds for different asset classes. For example, the fund could include a FTSE UK All Share Index fund, the FTSE Developed World ex-UK Equity Index fund, an emerging market index fund and corporate and government bond index funds. These underlying funds could be ETFs or they could be regular funds.

For an active ready-made fund, the overall fund manager will want specialist fund managers for each sector. It is unlikely that a specialist in emerging market equity will have above average expertise in the selection of corporate bonds. So, the typical active ready-made fund will comprise a dozen or more sub-mandates to cover the range of asset classes. Some funds will have up to two or three fund managers per asset class, to cover different investing styles and/or to provide optionality should the overall manager lose confidence in the strategy or operation of any one manager.

PASSIVE READY-MADE FUNDS

The two key competitors in the passive ready-made investing space are the global fund giants, Vanguard and Blackrock. Remember that no ready-made fund is completely passive. The fund manager is making an active choice as to the asset allocation but using passive fund building blocks to invest in each of the chosen assets.

Vanguard is the firm founded by the legendary Jack Bogle, who is credited with creating the world's first index fund. They offer a range of 5 ready-made funds called LifeStrategy Funds, ranging from 20% to 100% equity with the balance in bonds, and the 100% equity fund being the highest risk, highest reward fund. The funds are well diversified, with Vanguard saying that each fund holds between 6,000 to 20,000 shares and holds a spread of developed and emerging markets assets. The fees across the range are a low 0.22%. Of course, you need to pay a platform to hold this fund for you and this could cost anything from 0.15% to 0.45%, but it does mean that for less than 0.5% in fees you can have a fully diversified ready-made investment. Each fund is constructed from a number of underlying Vanguard index funds representing particular sectors or markets. For example, the LifeStrategy 60% equity fund has the following funds as its top 10 investments (as of July 2021):

Vanguard FTSE Developed World ex-UK Equity Index Fund	19.5%
Vanguard Global Bond Index Fund	19.1%
Vanguard FTSE UK All Share Index Unit Trust	14.7%
Vanguard US Equity Index Fund	14.7%
Vanguard UK Government Bond Index Fund	5.5%
Vanguard Emerging Markets Stock Index Fund	5.4%
Vanguard UK Inflation-Linked Gilt Index Fund	3.7%
Vanguard UK Investment Grade Bond Index Fund	3.4%
Vanguard FTSE Developed Europe ex-UK Equity Index Fund	3.3%
Vanguard Global Aggregate Bond ETF	3.0%

Table 2: *Vanguard LifeStrategy 60% top 10 investments*

The LifeStrategy funds are popular with almost £20bn invested in the UK range[19]:

	Total assets
LifeStrategy 20% equity fund	£2.3bn
LifeStrategy 40% equity fund	£7.9bn
LifeStrategy 60% equity fund	£12.5bn
LifeStrategy 80% equity fund	£6.5bn
Lifestrategy 100% equity fund	£3.4bn
Total	£32.6bn

Table 3: AuM in Vanguard LifeStrategy UK range

The spread of investor choice across the range is not surprising and mirrors the spread found across other risk-profiled fund ranges. The classic 60/40 equity bond fund has an enduring appeal to investors. Though perhaps this is also because if you offer a choice of five funds, many will go for the middle option, thinking that must be the most sensible choice! A more rational explanation is that older investors are richer (it takes a long time to accumulate wealth), and older investors are generally more risk-averse in their investing for good reason – they have less time to recover from market shocks and need their investments for income now or very soon. Of course, we know that for the younger, long-term investor, it's often the better choice to take on more risk.

Blackrock is the world's largest asset manager, and also the largest issuer of ETFs in the world with its iShares range, which now have over $2 trillion in assets[20]. They offer a range of 4 ready-made funds called the MyMap range (they also share with Vanguard a fondness for concatenated fund names with a capital letter part way through!). The range, somewhat unusually, starts with MyMap3 as the most conservative (least risky) and has 4 risk-profiled funds with MyMap6 being the most equity heavy of the range. This range was launched in May 2019, and priced at just 0.17%, undercutting Vanguard by a significant margin. Blackrock's approach to asset allocation is different to Vanguard's in two respects: (1) Rather than committing to a fixed equity allocation for each profile, it's targeting a volatility range for each profile. (2) It's not limiting its fund managers to just equity and bonds but includes 'alternative' assets such as commodities and real estate in the asset allocation.

The asset allocations are as follows (as of December 2020):

Fund	Bonds	Equities	Alternatives	Vol Targets
MyMap3	75%	20%	5%	3–6%
MyMap4	52%	43%	5%	6–9%
MyMap5	33%	62%	5%	8–11%
MyMap6	16%	79%	5%	10–15%

Table 4: Blackrock MyMap asset allocation

Each fund is constructed from a number of underlying Blackrock iShares ETFs, representing a particular sector or market.

For example, the MyMap5 fund is made up of the following funds (as of July 2021):

Name	Weight (%)
iShares MSCI US ESG Enhanced ETF	18.26
iShares North American Equity Index Fund	12.16
iShares MSCI EMU (Europe) ESG Enhanced ETF	10.95
iShares $ Treasury Bond 20+yr ETF	9.22
iShares 100 UK Equity Index Fund	7.97
iShares US 'TIPS' (Inflation protected treasury bond) ETF	6.05
iShares US Equity Index Fund	6.05
iShares MSCI EM ESG Enhanced ETF	6.02
iShares Treasury Bond ETF	5.07
iShares Index Linked Gilt Index Fund	4.01

Table 5: *Blackrock MyMap5 investments*

Given the range is relatively new, it has a far smaller investor base than Vanguard's LifeStrategy range, with around £500m invested at this stage.

So which of these two should you choose? LifeStrategy has the advantage of being simple, you know what you are getting and it has a long track record. Ordinary investors may well struggle to be excited by the technicalities of MyMap's 'volatility targeting'. However, the MyMap range has the advantage of a wider asset allocation pallet, which may provide more of a cushion in drawdown. Though, investors who want 100% equity will be frustrated at the ~80% equity allocation of MyMap 6, the range's most aggressive fund – they may well prefer the LifeStrategy 100% equity fund.

One further difference between the two funds is the approach to asset allocation. LifeStrategy broadly allocates on the basis of relative market size, with an overweighting in the UK (~ 25% UK equity in LifeStrategy 100). Vanguard takes the view that UK investors will want more exposure to UK assets. This 'home bias' is not unusual: many other UK asset managers take a similar approach. With MyMap, Blackrock uses a more dynamic, scientific process to determine the asset allocation (to manage within the target volatility bands), and this also impacts its allocations across markets.

Interestingly Blackrock has a range of funds that take a similar approach to LifeStrategy, and it's called the Blackrock Consensus range. It would seem the promotion of these funds is being ramped down in favour of the MyMap range. Despite the similarities between the two funds, the Consensus range never got the traction that LifeStrategy did, and it would appear that Blackrock feels they need to take a different approach (and lower pricing) to capture market share from Vanguard.

These are both high-quality products from major asset managers with huge credibility, and both at very low costs, so it's hard to see that there would be a big difference in outcomes from either option. So, probably, it comes down to which approach makes more sense to you. Of course, we need more time to see the relative performance of the two options, and, even then, as we know, allocation outcomes are more luck than skill.

Of course, there are other similar ready-made passive products out there. Barclays Wealth has its 'Global Markets' range, from 1 (least volatile, lowest equity content) to 5 (close to 100% equity). This uses the same active asset allocation that Barclays uses for its private client portfolio, with the underlying funds being in ETFs. So, the asset allocation is more active than

LifeStrategy, and the fund has a longer track record than MyMap, though costs are 0.45%. Similarly, Abrdn has its MyFolio Market range (what is this obsession with concatenated names with a capital letter part way through?), similarly ranging from (i) to (v), with costs at around 0.3% across the profiles. Other similar ranges from big names include Fidelity's 'Cost Focus' portfolios and the HSBC Global Strategy Portfolios. Most of these funds are promoted through advisors or through the firm's own in-house platforms or advisory businesses, so don't get the same profile as the Vanguard and Blackrock offerings. You can generally find them to buy through DIY platforms, but you may have to dig a bit harder to get the information.

An alternative approach that has gained traction with DIY investors in search of simple, easy-to-use low-cost solutions is just to buy a global index fund. The MSCI ACWI (All Country All World) Index tracks about 3000 large- and medium-sized firms in 23 developed markets and 27 emerging markets and covers 85% of the total value of all the shares listed across the globe. In this sort of fund, the fund manager has put no thought into the asset allocation. You just get the allocation of the index. So, it's not really a ready-made fund like LifeStrategy or MyMap, but it is reasonably well diversified across markets and sectors. The US market includes some very large and valuable firms so ends up making up about 55% of the MSCI ACWI index. Of course, many of these large US firms have a significant share of their revenue coming from outside of the US (e.g., Apple has around 60% of its revenue from non-US sources[21]), so this is less of an issue than it might appear. This only works if you want a 100% equity profile. If you want a lower risk equity/bond mix you will need to buy a diversified bond fund and blend the two.

ESG READY-MADE FUNDS

At the time of writing, there is just one passive ready-made fund available to retail investors and that's the Blackrock MyMap 5 Select ESG Fund. And yes, there is just one risk profile, 5, which has around 64% equity. This fund was launched in June 2020, so there is a limited performance history. It's made up of investments in Blackrock's iShares, 80% of which are subject to ESG requirements. Blackrock launched this product with what they know to be the most popular risk profile (closest to a classic 60/40 equity/bond portfolio). Pricing is the same as for the other MyMap funds, just 0.17%. I am told that Blackrock will extend this range and the remainder of the profiles will be available in due course.

One alternative, if you are aiming for 100% equity exposure, is to buy a global ESG ETF. Blackrock's iShares has a set of ESG funds based on the MSCI World, the global index covering developed market shares. They have three levels of ESG 'intensity'. The lowest is the iShares MSCI World ESG Screened ETF, where certain controversial businesses are screened out (e.g., weapons, tobacco, thermal coal). The next one up is the iShares MSCI World ESG Enhanced ETF – where, in addition to screening out controversial businesses, greater weighting is given to companies with higher ESG scores. Finally, there is the iShares MSCI World ESG SRI ETF which, in addition to screening out controversial businesses, selects companies in the top 25% of each sector based on their ESG scores. All three of these products cost 0.2% so are at a similar price point to the LifeStrategy and MyMap ranges. If you decide to invest in one of these funds as your ready-made fund you need to be aware the exposure is to developed market shares only. Typically, other ready-made funds will have around an 8-10% allocation to emerging market shares, so not having this exposure won't make a huge difference, but you need to be aware that you are losing this dimension.

If you like the ESG index fund option just described, but don't want to be 100% exposed to equity, then an option is to blend your MSCI ESG fund with the Blackrock MyMap 5 Select ESG Fund. Given MyMap 5 is around 60% equity, a 50/50 blend will leave you with an 80/20 equity/bond portfolio.

ACTIVE ESG FUNDS

As we said earlier, one of the only reasons to invest in an active fund, is because of the limited choice for ESG investors in low-cost ready-made investments. There is no equivalent ESG option to the Vanguard LifeStrategy range and just the one risk profile (MyMap 5) for the Blackrock MyMap range. The only full range of passive options are via robo-advisors and cost just over 1% in fees. This will change; ESG investing is still a relatively recent development and every month there are new ESG offerings. For now, I am highlighting two prominent active ready-made ESG fund ranges that are worth considering.

The first is from Liontrust, an asset manager with a long track record in sustainable investing. They offer a range of five 'Sustainable Future (SF)' risk-profiled managed funds. They have had these funds risk profiled by independent 3rd parties, Distribution Technology (using their 'Dynamic Planner' model) and Defaqto.

Fund	Dynamic Planner Risk Profile	Defaqto Risk Profile	Equity allocation %
SF Defensive Managed	4	3	20–50
SF Cautious Managed	5	4	40–60
SF Managed	6	6	60–85
SF Managed Growth	7	7	60–100
SF Global Growth	8	9	90–100

Table 6: Liontrust Sustainable Futures range

The full range has a 5-year track record and the Managed, Managed Growth and Global Growth have a 10-year record. Liontrust makes the claim that the performance of these funds is in the top quartile of performance in their respective sectors over three and five years to the end of June 2021 and three funds that have been around that long are in the top quartile over the 10 years to June 2021. The OCF is 0.87-0.89%, which if you combine it with the platform fee charged by one of the cheaper platforms at, say, 0.2% will result in a total all-in fee of just over 1%. That is not much more than the costs of a passive robo-advisor's portfolio, and certainly cheaper than an active robo-advisor.

The second active ESG fund range is from Royal London. It would seem this range has been set up for sale via financial advisors, so less information is available to the retail investor. But you can find the range on DIY platforms, and the effective pricing at 0.76-0.77% (OCF) is lower than Liontrust's. You will be able to find the fund fact sheets and a brochure on the range on the internet. The total combined platform and fund fees for this range would come to less than 1% (assuming 0.2% platform costs), so just cheaper than a passive robo-portfolio.

Fund	Dynamic Planner Risk profile	Equity benchmark range %
RL Sustainable Managed Income	4	0
RL Sustainable Managed Growth	4	0–35
RL Sustainable Diversified	5	20–60
RL Sustainable World	7	40–85
RL Sustainable Leaders	8	Up to 100

Table 7: Royal London Sustainable range

Note that the 'Sustainable Leaders' fund invests mostly in UK companies, so is not actually a diversified fund. Royal London is a mutual, i.e., has no shareholders, with profit ploughed back into the business or rebated to unit holders. This does impact the culture and dynamic of the firm and they would say aligns them more naturally to sustainable objectives as a firm.

For all sustainable funds you need to read the brochures and make sure you understand the ESG screening approach. There is no point in paying a premium for an ESG product only to find that you are unconvinced by the effectiveness of their approach. Equally you should do your own research into the performance track record and investment approach of any of these active funds or active robos. Investing in active funds is about picking a winning fund or at least avoiding a fund that materially lags the market.

With any active product it's not advisable to place your entire portfolio with one manager. Of course, with a ready-made product the 'high-conviction' ideas are moderated by the diversification across multiple sectors and markets so you don't run as much risk as you would with a single sector fund. However, you are still reliant on one team for the tactical asset allocation calls and appointment of the underlying managers. When these calls go the right way and the market moves as they say it will, then there will be outperformance. But of course when the market goes against their strategy then you will underperform the index and could lose money. With a single sector fund (e.g., UK large-cap equity) the advice is generally to limit each active fund to no more than 10% of your holdings. For a well-diversified ready-made fund, perhaps spread your portfolio across two or three funds if you can. For a passive fund, this is less of an issue given the only difference between funds is the asset allocation, so you can just buy one fund. However, there is no harm in spreading your investment 50/50 across a couple of providers and effectively getting a blend of the two asset allocation approaches.

THE ROBO-ADVISOR OPTION FOR ESG

There are over 10 robo-advisors operating in the UK markets at any one time. And I use the phrase 'at any one time' deliberately; many haven't lasted very long and others are too new to be sure they will last. It's a fashionable business to be in: cutting-edge technology making investing easier. But it's not profitable at all (yet). Nutmeg, one of the earliest entrants to this market reported losses of over £21m for the 2019 financial year, for income of just £9m (though that didn't deter JP Morgan, the US bank, from paying a reported £700m to buy Nutmeg in 2021). And it's not just start-ups that struggle with this; UBS, a major global bank, asset and wealth manager shut down its robo-advice business less than 2 years after launch. Investec, another international banking and wealth management firm, shut its robo-advisor in 2019, losing over £32m in the 2-year experiment.

So future longevity is a key factor in choosing a robo-advisor. Of course, 'client money' rules mean you shouldn't lose your investment if your robo-advisor goes bankrupt. The FCA has strict rules to ensure all investment firms keep client assets and money separate from firm money so in the event of insolvency your investments are safe from the creditors of the investment firm. Also, until now, these firms have wound down in an orderly fashion, and have made arrangements to transfer client investments to others. But it's a hassle to have to move to a new provider and you don't want your investments to be managed by a firm that's focused on short-term survival and may not be around for the long-term.

A key reason to use a robo-advisor is the lack of options for investing in a ready-made passive ESG portfolio. The ESG market is still in its infancy and there isn't a full range of ready-made passive funds out there. However, there is a full range of passive ESG ETFs covering different sectors and some of the robo-advisors have built ready-made diversified ESG portfolios for their clients using these ETFs as their building blocks.

There are two prominent robo-advisors who offer ESG portfolios with passive underlying holdings: Nutmeg and Moneyfarm. A 3rd robo-advisor, Wealthify also provides ESG portfolios (their Ethical Plan option); however, their portfolios use active underlying funds.

Robo-advisor	Charges[22]
Nutmeg Socially Responsible Portfolio	~1.02% of assets (0.75% fee on 1st £100k, and 0.35% on the portion above £100k + ~0.27% underlying funds costs)
Moneyfarm Socially Responsible Portfolios	Up to 1.04% of assets (0.75% fee below £10k reducing on a stepped scale down to 0.35% for amounts over £100k + ~0.2% underlying funds costs + 0.09% spread)
Wealthify Ethical Plan (active funds)	~ 1.3% of assets (0.6% fee + ~0.7% underlying funds costs for ethical funds)

It is important to note that of the three providers, only Nutmeg offers a Lifetime ISA, so if you plan to invest into a LISA (which I believe you should do if you can), then neither of the other two robo-advisors are suitable.

Nutmeg was one of the UK's earlier robo-advisors and has been going since 2011. It's also one of the UK's largest robo-advisors with around £3.5bn in assets under management (AuM). In June 2021 it was announced that JP Morgan, the US bank, had agreed to buy Nutmeg. Moneyfarm was started in Italy in 2012 and in the UK in 2016 and has around £1.9bn AuM. While Wealthify started out as an independent stand-alone start-up, it is now wholly owned by Aviva, one of the UK's largest insurance and investment firms.

MAKE YOUR CHOICE

I have taken you through a lot of options above. The purpose is to give you a good overview of the landscape so once you have made your choice you feel confident in the choice(s) that you have made. However, I realise there is a risk that having this much information can be paralysing and slows down the decision. Any of these choices is better than doing nothing, so don't overthink it but make a decision and move on. If it helps you make the decision, hedge your bets and choose a couple of funds. Once you have been at it for a while, you can always sell out of one of them and consolidate.

YOUR WORKPLACE PENSION

If you are employed and enrolled in your company's pension plan, you will usually be given the option to choose the fund that your pension pot is invested in. If you don't make a choice, you will be invested in a default fund, often a balanced fund (around 60/40 equity/bond allocation). This default fund may be completely unsuitable for you. If you have just started work and have a long investment horizon, a balanced fund is unlikely to be right for you. Also, the fund costs may be high. The choice will usually be from a limited list, and unfortunately may not include familiar names or funds, so you may well need to do a bit of work. Essentially, look for a well-diversified fund, low cost (index funds or 'trackers') and make sure it is sufficiently equity rich to match your risk tolerance. If you don't recall having ever made an investment choice for your pension, then don't delay. Check the position now and make the changes right away.

In summary:
- The two key competitors in the passive ready-made investing space are the global fund giants Vanguard and Blackrock.
- Vanguard's offers the LifeStrategy range of 5 ready-made funds ranging from 20% to 100% equity.

- Blackrock has a range of 4 funds from MyMap3 with ~25% equity to MyMap 6 with ~80% equity.
- Many other wealth and asset management firms also offer passive ready-made funds.
- Currently there is only one passive ESG ready-made fund, and that is the ESG variant of MyMap5 (~60% equity).
- Otherwise, investors will need to choose a global index ESG ETF (for 100% equity exposure), an active ESG fund or invest via one of the robo-advisors who offer passive ESG portfolios.

8

CHOOSING A PLATFORM AND BUYING YOUR INVESTMENT

PUTTING IT ALL TOGETHER

Unless you are going with a robo-advisor you will need to choose a 'platform' to buy and hold your fund. Most fund managers don't want to be in the business of dealing with lots of retail customers and providing them with the ability to buy and sell their funds and track their existing holdings. So, for DIY investors, funds are distributed through investment platforms, sometimes also referred to as fund supermarkets.

There are over a dozen investment platforms out there and most of them have more than enough functionality to do what you need them to do if you are buying a ready-made fund, and most provide a good service, so it largely comes down to cost. And given the fee structures are different across providers, being a mix of a % of the assets under management, fixed and/or minimum fees, the cheapest provider for you will depend on the size of your portfolio.

Platforms also charge for other things like buying and selling funds and reinvesting dividends. If you limit your transactions to just regular investing, for most platforms this won't amount to much.

To simplify the cost comparison, I have shown below total costs for a portfolio with a fund worth £20k or £100k from the major providers, sourced from the Lang Cat,[23] industry researchers and consultants. Of course, this is a simplified representation and charges change from time to time, so, before you pick a platform, make sure you understand their charges. In particular, if you intend to invest a regular monthly amount and will have less than £20k to start, the cheapest deal is likely to be from a platform with a % of assets charge and no fixed fee or minimum. Of course, at £20k and less, they are all pretty cheap, with most of them less than £5 per month, and none of them are making very much money off you. They make their money off the frequent traders and the larger portfolios.

Platform	LISA	Cost for £20k		Cost for £100k	
		%	£pa	%	£pa
AJ Bell Youinvest	✓	0.28	56	0.26	256
Barclays Smart Investor		0.30	60	0.21	212
Charles Stanley Direct		0.35	70	0.35	350
Fidelity		0.35	70	0.35	350
Halifax Share Dealing		0.37	63	0.07	63
Hargreaves Lansdown	✓	0.45	90	0.45	450

Platform	LISA	Cost for £20k		Cost for £100k	
HSBC InvestDirect		0.25	50	0.25	250
Interactive Investor		0.60	120	0.12	120
Vanguard		0.15	30	0.15	150

Table 8: Platform costs

Only two providers currently offer a LISA: AJ Bell and Hargreaves Lansdown. All of the platforms offer SIPPs and regular ISAs. While the LISA product has only been around a few years, it's been rumoured for some time that the government will scrap it (because it's such a good deal!), so the other platforms are reluctant to invest in the build required to offer it. For most people, if you are eligible to invest in a LISA you should, so you then only have these two platforms to choose from. Of the two, AJ Bell is the cheapest. Hargreaves Lansdown is one of the most expensive platforms out there. Of course price isn't everything and the quality of service and platform functionality also matters. However, ready-made investing doesn't need a lot of functionality.

Also note that Vanguard only offers its own products, which is fine if you are convinced by their LifeStrategy funds and don't intend to invest elsewhere, but you will need to switch platforms if you change your mind.

SHARE CLASSES

When buying funds, you need to have some understanding of fund share classes and the difference between Income and Accumulation units within each share class.

For most funds there will be the option of buying the 'Inc' or the 'Acc' option for each share class (Income or Accumulation). The income option will pay out any income generated by the underlying investments, i.e., dividends from the shares, or coupons from the bonds or interest on cash. For some funds the income option is labelled 'distributing'. The accumulation option will automatically reinvest the income back into the fund. If you need the income from the fund, then it may make sense to buy the income version, but otherwise it's better to buy the accumulation version and benefit from the compounding effect of reinvesting.

You could just ask your platform to reinvest any income you receive back into the fund, as you would need to do for the dividends from any direct equities you hold. However, that may be more costly. The platform may well charge a transaction fee for each reinvestment trade.

Note that unless the fund is held within a tax-sheltered wrapper, like a LISA/ISA or SIPP, the income will be taxable if in total the amounts are above the tax-free dividend and interest allowances. If you hold the income option, you will see the amounts paid out, whereas with the accumulation unit you will need to refer to the 'notional distribution' statement that your platform should provide you with. These amounts also affect the Capital Gains Tax (CGT) payable. With income units this is a simple calculation, as the current value of your holding, less what you paid when you originally bought it, will be the capital gain. With the accumulation units, you need to deduct the notional income accumulated over the time you have held the fund from the current unit value before calculating the capital gain. If you don't do this, you will overpay the CGT.

Fund managers typically issue each fund in four, five or even more share classes. The share classes have different letters associated with them, but there is no industry convention as to what these letters mean so you need to work it out for each fund.

Often a fund will have a share class for larger institutional investors such as pension funds. The fees for this share class will be much lower as essentially this is the fund manager giving a 'bulk discount' to larger investors. This share class will not be available on any of the retail platforms, though you may see it referenced in the fund manager's literature, or on the Morningstar or Trustnet sites, the investment fund research information providers.

Funds may have different share classes to allow an investor to choose to be hedged or unhedged for currency fluctuations. An example of this is where the underlying investments are in US dollars and the investor wants to be protected from the £/$ fluctuations. Generally, for long-term investors the recommendation is not to hedge – it adds quite a bit to costs and you could end up losing out if the pound weakens. If your horizon is short, it is worth considering, but you do need to know (1) what you are doing and (2) the costs and risk of the two alternatives.

If you have had a fund investment for a long time, it's worth checking that you don't have a 'pre-RDR' share class. Prior to 2013, it was common for fund managers to pay financial advisors trail commission on funds they sold or advised on. So, a proportion of the annual charge for the fund was then paid to the advisor's firm. In 2013, as a result of the 'Retail Distribution Review' (RDR), the FCA banned trail commission. Advisor firms now need to levy a discrete and transparent charge for advice and fund managers introduced new, cheaper share classes without the trail charge. However, legacy trail arrangements were allowed to carry on. While some firms have moved clients to the cheaper 'post-RDR' share classes, others haven't. So, if you have fund investments that predate 2013, it's important that you check you are getting a fair deal.

Some fund managers will agree on a discounted share class with a particular platform. This is controversial, as there have been cases where it's been alleged that certain platforms only promote funds that have agreed on a share class discount with them. Of course, the platform doesn't benefit from the share class discount directly, but by persuading potential customers that it has negotiated a good deal with popular fund providers, more will invest through their platform and their revenues will go up. This practice can lead to a situation where a platform's 'best buy' fund list is being driven by the platform's commercial interest, and not objective investment considerations.

In reality, this is less complex to navigate than you might imagine. When you buy a fund through a platform you will typically be presented with just the one applicable share class with the option to go with either the income or the accumulation units within that share class. It's only when you search for fund information outside of the platform that you will need to understand that there are other share classes, and make sure any information or research is applicable to the share class you hold or plan to buy.

FUND FACTS

Your investment platform will always provide you with a document called a Key Information Document (KID) and almost always with a Fund Factsheet as well. (Note the KID used to be called a KIID, and some sites still use the longer acronym).

It's a regulatory requirement that they provide you with a KID before you invest in a fund and there are strict requirements for what must be in the KID. It covers the fund's essential features including the fund's charges, its risk and reward profile and past performance. The fund's risk and reward is categorised across a standardised seven-point scale. Included in the KID are overall costs of the fund in the form of the 'ongoing charges figure' (OCF). This includes the fund's 'annual management charge' (AMC) and a variety of other operating costs, though importantly it excludes the trading costs incurred by the fund. More active funds will have higher trading costs, but currently it's not easy to work out what they are. The FCA is reviewing fund charges and transparency and hopefully this will improve so that the full costs are clear to the investor.

The Fund Factsheet is a more user-friendly overview that's designed to help you decide if you want to invest in the fund. It typically provides information such as the fund's investment objective, asset allocation, top 10 holdings and how it has performed in the past. There is some overlap between the KID and the factsheet, but it's best to read both to make sure you fully understand what it is you are investing in.

There will be separate versions of the KID and Factsheet for each share class and for the income and accumulation options. You will also find the unique identifier for the fund in the form of an ISIN (International Securities Identification Number), SEDOL (Stock Exchange Daily Official List) etc. The KID and the fact sheet can also be found on other investor information sites, such as Trustnet and Morningstar and these sites provide additional information and analytical services that may be useful in your fund research.

In summary:
- Unless you are investing through a robo-advisor, you will need to choose a platform to buy and hold your ready-made fund.

- There are over a dozen platforms out there and most of them have all the functionality you will need, so the choice is mostly a matter of cost.

- However, if you are investing through a LISA, note that only a few platforms offer this. Also be aware that the Vanguard's platform is restricted to its own products.

- For most funds you will have the choice between the Income (Inc) and Accumulation (Acc) share classes, where the Inc class pays out all income and the Acc reinvests income back into the fund.

- You will often save reinvesting transaction costs by holding the Acc class. However, if your holdings are outside of a tax wrapper and you need to pay tax on the income and gains, the Inc class can make it easier to do the tax calculations.

- Your platform is required to provide a Key Information Document (KID) for your investment and will almost always provide a Fund Factsheet as well. Importantly, included in the KID are the fund's 'ongoing charges figure' (OCF).

9

INVESTING ENOUGH AND THE 4% RULE

So how much do you need to save for financial independence or retirement? Well, that depends on how much income you want when you stop working. This chapter will explain the 4% rule and why it is useful in working out the size of the pot you will need to save towards (your 'number'). I will also show you how to build a basic spreadsheet as a guide to how much you should save to reach your 'number'.

THE 4% RULE

So how much is enough? Well, if you are saving for retirement or financial independence you need to know about the '4% rule'. The 4% rule says you can sustainably withdraw 4% of your portfolio each year in retirement and not run out of money. It's ascribed to William Bengen, a Californian rocket engineer turned financial advisor, who published his research in 1994 in the (US) *Journal of Financial Planning*. Using actual returns for a 50/50 equity bond portfolio from the prior 75 years, he established that retirees who draw down no more than 4.2% of their portfolio in the initial year and adjust that amount for inflation each subsequent year would not outlive their money over a 30-year retirement. He updated his research in 2012, in the wake of the 2008 crisis and found his rule still held. The rule assumes a moderate-risk portfolio in retirement; there may be insufficient time to recover from the deep losses from a higher-risk equity-only portfolio.

There is some controversy on this percentage and it has been suggested that 3.5% or even 3% may now be more appropriate given that in general yields have come down so much since the 2008 crisis. At what age you start drawing your pension is also a factor – if you are going to start drawing your pension at state pension age, currently 66 but eventually going up to 68, then 4% may well be fine. If you start drawing down at 55 and need your money to last another decade or so, you may need to be more conservative and go with 3.5% or even 3%. Of course, your chosen asset allocation makes a difference. If you go for a high proportion of bonds in your portfolio, you will have to go for a lower withdrawal rate, but there is less risk of failure.

Much of what's been written on the 4% rule is from a US perspective. While of course UK investors shouldn't have only UK assets in their portfolios, and there's no reason they should not be able to enjoy similar returns to US investors, there are some practical constraints. Fortunately, there is a book on this written from a UK perspective, *Beyond the 4% rule: The science of retirement portfolios that last a lifetime* by Abraham Okusanya. Okusanya is the CEO of a start-up that provides software to financial planners answering these very questions for their clients. In the book, he makes the important point that the original Bengen rule was based on periods of extreme crisis, such as the crash of 1929 and two world wars. Despite the upheavals of recent decades, we haven't seen this sort of impact on investor portfolios for quite some time. He also notes that Bengen's analysis was based on a quite inflexible withdrawal approach. By making small, sensible adjustments as circumstances change, such as not increasing your income by inflation in the year immediately after a market reversal, you can significantly increase the probability of success of your sustainable drawdown strategy.

So 4%, while not perfect, is a good starting point for your plan. If you have £1m you can plan on drawing up to £40,000 each year. If you think £40,000 is enough for you then the 'number' you need to save towards is £1m in today's money. Bear in mind that you may have other sources of income such as a state pension. Clearly you will need to make some adjustment for inflation, as by the time you get to your retirement age that £40,000 will need to be more, given the cost of living will have gone up.

SACRIFICE SPENDING TODAY

Of course, to save for tomorrow, you have to sacrifice spending today. Investment is all about delayed gratification. The textbook definition of investment is deferral of current consumption for future consumption. And if you are not saving enough, you are going to have to spend less (or earn more) so you can save more.

In 2015, a story hit the press of a man from Vermont in the US, who died aged 92 leaving an estate worth $8m. The reason there was a story was that the man, Ronald Read, worked for 25 years as an attendant and a mechanic at the local fuel station and later became a caretaker at a department store, a career not considered likely to make you a multi-millionaire. But he lived a very frugal life, driving an old used car, living in a modest house, with wood chopping, and stamp and coin collecting as his hobbies, and he invested his spare cash in a well-diversified portfolio of 'blue-chip' shares (shares of well-established companies). After leaving $2 million to his stepchildren, caregivers, and friends, he left $4.8 million to his local hospital and $1.2 million to a library. Both bequests were the largest donations the institutions had ever received.

You may have heard of the 'FIRE' movement – 'Financial Independence Retire Early'. Its adherents typically save 50–75% of their income to reach the goal of retiring in their 30s and 40s. It's mostly a US phenomenon, but it has its adherents in the UK. For most of us with 'normal' lives it's probably going a bit far – less delayed gratification, more enduring extreme hardship. And it seems the successful ones don't so much retire early as switch career to writing smug blogs about retiring early. But there are some good lessons in these blogs about keeping your expenses low and prioritising savings.

As Mr Micawber famously said in the novel by Charles Dickens, *David Copperfield*:

"*Annual income twenty pounds, annual expenditure nineteen and six, result happiness. Annual income twenty pounds, annual expenditure twenty pounds ought and six, result misery.*"

So how much should you save? It's generally recommended you aim to save around 15% of your pre-tax income. That's a good rule of thumb if you are in your 20s, but of course there are too many variables for a rule of thumb like this to be relied upon. It's easy enough to build a spreadsheet to work out a simple savings and investment plan, as I show you later in this chapter.

FUTURE RETURNS

As you save, how fast will your money grow? Of course, we don't know how much assets will grow in the future, but we do know the historical returns of stocks and bonds over a number of years. Credit Suisse publishes a *Global Investment Returns Yearbook* authored by Elroy Dimson, Paul Marsh and Mike Staunton. In this, they publish their calculations of the historic average real returns for equities and long-term government bonds for a number of markets. In the 2021 Yearbook[24] they show that UK equities have returned an average of 5.4% over the window 1900 to 2020. For 1971 to 2020, it's higher at 6.3%, while for 2001 to 2020, it's only 2.5%. Though, of course, the 'dot-com' bubble and the Covid-19 epidemic bracketed the 2001 to 2020 window which has skewed the returns for this window. UK government bonds have returned a real average of 2% since 1900, 4.7% since 1971 and 4.4% since 2001. For the US equities have returned a real average of 6.6% since 1900, 6.7% since 1971 and 6% since 2001 and government bonds have returned 2% since 1900, 4.3% since 1971 and 4.8% since 2001. You may be surprised by the high returns on bonds since 2000, given the very low yields on bonds in recent years. But, of course, since 2000 as yields have come down the prices of bonds have gone up leaving investors in these bonds with large asset price gains. Going forward, bond yields are so low that arguably the headroom for further asset growth from them going even lower is limited. The yield on UK 10-year government bonds is around 0.85% at the time of writing, and with arguably no room for asset price growth from rates falling, and risk of rates rising – so overall bond returns could well be negative over the next few years.

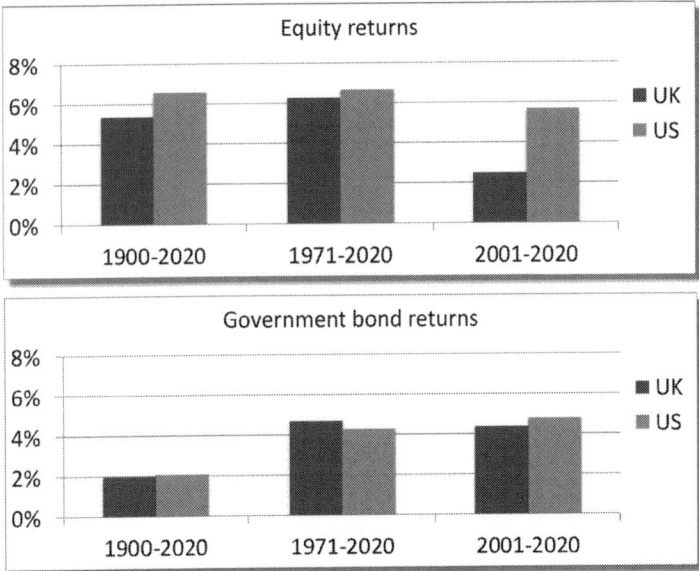

Figure 5: Historic investment returns[25]

So realistically you are unlikely to get much more than a 6% real return from a 100%-equity portfolio going forward, and possibly as low as 4%. Should you be going for less than 100% equity in your portfolio, returns will be more muted over the long-term, though your 'ready-made' 60/40 or 80/20 portfolio will comprise only a small proportion of lower-yielding government bonds, with the balance made up of higher-yielding corporate bonds, and possibly some real estate or even some emerging market bonds. But you will need to plan on less than 4% real return for a 60/40 or 80/20 portfolio.

What do I mean by 'real' rate of return? A real rate of return is the rate of return above inflation, whereas the 'nominal' return is the total return including inflation.

Nominal return = real return + inflation.

So if your portfolio grows by 6% and inflation is 2% then your portfolio has only grown by 4% in real terms[26].

Inflation eats away at the purchasing power of money. If inflation is 2% then we need £102 this year to buy the basket of goods that cost us £100 last year. For some time, governments have prioritised keeping inflation low, and currently the Bank of England is targeted with keeping inflation at around 2%. This doesn't sound like much, but over time, with compounding, it can amount to quite a bit. As a long-term investor, with a 2% annual inflation rate over 20 years the purchasing power of £100 will decline to £67. That's around a third of your money eaten up by inflation.

For planning purposes it's simpler to work with the real rate of return.

PUTTING IT ALL TOGETHER

If you are saving to have £1m (in today's money) by the time you retire, you should build a simple spreadsheet that looks something like this:

I have cheated and made sure this works (just) so that at 60, the target retirement pot is reached, but of course you will have to fiddle around to do this and will have to make real-life adjustments, like saving more, to make this work.

If you are in a couple, you may choose to do this together or individually, that depends on how you work things between you, but either way you do need to look at the combined output so you can both agree on the target and the sacrifices to get there.

Don't forget to include your company pension contributions.

I think it's simplest if you calculate everything in today's money (i.e., without adding inflation) and then use real rates

Current investments			Investment growth forecast		
ISA:	£30,000		Age	Savings	Total investment
Pension:	£50,000		34	£8,000	£102,900
Other:	£10,000		35	£8,320	£116,781
Total:	£90,000		36	£8,653	£131,705
			37	£8,999	£147,740
			38	£9,359	£164,953
			39	£9,733	£183,421
Required retirement pot calculation			40	£10,123	£203,221
Target withdrawal rate:	4%		41	£10,527	£224,436
Total income required:	£50,000		42	£10,949	£247,153
Income from state/other pension:	£8,000		43	£11,386	£271,467
Net income required:	£42,000		44	£11,842	£297,474
Required retirement pot:	£1,050,000		45	£12,316	£325,279
			46	£12,808	£354,992
			47	£13,321	£386,728
Savings plan			48	£13,853	£420,611
Annual savings (incl Pension & ISA):	8000		49	£14,408	£456,769
Real growth in annual savings:	4%		50	£14,984	£495,341
Estimated real return on investments:	5%		51	£15,583	£536,470
			52	£16,207	£580,310
			53	£16,855	£627,023
			54	£17,529	£676,780
			55	£18,230	£729,761
			56	£18,959	£786,156
			57	£19,718	£846,167
			58	£20,506	£910,008
			59	£21,327	£977,901
			60	£22,180	£1,050,085

Figure 6: Investment planning spreadsheet

of return. So if you have worked out you need to save £1m for retirement in today's money (using the current, rather than the future, inflation adjusted value of money), then use that sum in your spreadsheet, but then ensure you use real rates of return and don't add inflation to any of the figures (i.e., your salary). But then if your plan is to increase your savings rate over time, then ensure you do so in real, not nominal terms.

In the example spreadsheet on the previous page, we were working towards a £1m pot (in today's value of money) in 27 years' time, to have an additional income of £42k per year (in today's value of money). We use a real rate of return estimate of 5% and increase our savings by a real 4% each year (assuming our salary will go up by that amount each year as we progress). If inflation is 2%, then we actually need to increase our savings by 6%[27] each year in nominal terms.

THE POWER OF COMPOUNDING

When you start saving 'outweighs' how much you save. The size of your pot is a function of 3 factors: (1) how much you invest, (2) growth rate and (3) time. And time is really valuable because of the power of compounding. Compounding is the process whereby you reinvest your earnings each year, so the next year you have a larger base on which to build and your pot grows by even more. If you start with £100 and your portfolio

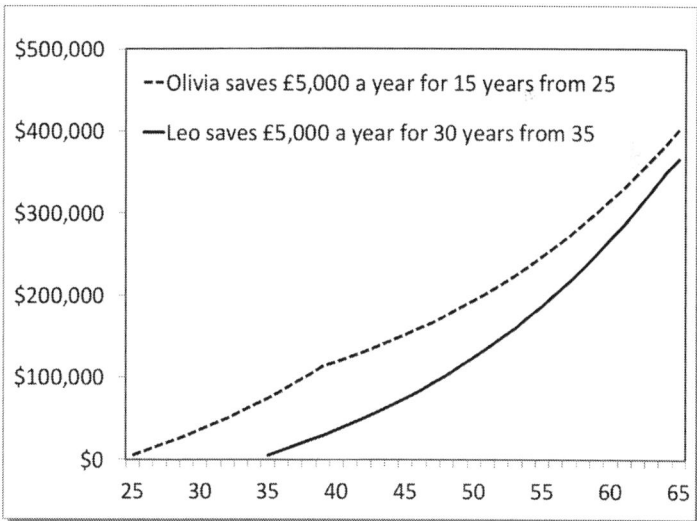

Figure 7: The power of compounding

grows at 6% every year after one year, it is worth £106. But the next year you get 6% on not just the £100, but also on the extra £6 you plough back into your investment account. After 5 years it's grown not by just £30 (6x5) but by £34, because of the bit of extra growth on the amount you reinvest each year. This growth on growth is exponential, so after 10 years it's grown by £79 and not just by £68 (2x34).

To illustrate the power of compounding over time, take the case of two investors, let's call them Olivia and Leo. Olivia invests £5,000 a year for 15 years from age 25 and then stops, but leaves her money invested until age 65. Leo only starts investing at 35 but keeps doing so until he is 65. So Olivia has invested a total of £75,000 and Leo has invested £150,000. However, assuming growth at 5%, at 65 Olivia has over £400,000 and Leo has only £366,000, despite investing twice as much.

In summary:
- We all need to take responsibility for calculating how big a fund we need for our retirement and take the risk that if we draw down too much of our savings in each year of retirement we will run out of money.
- A frequently used rule of thumb for sustainable retirement spending is the '4% rule'. It says you withdraw 4% of the value of your investments in the 1st year of retirement; in subsequent years, you adjust the amount you withdraw to account for inflation.
- To save for tomorrow, you need to sacrifice spending today; investment is all about delayed gratification.
- It is generally recommended to save around 15% of your pre-tax income to fund retirement.

- However, there are a number of variables, and it's best to work out how much you need to save to reach your goals by building a simple forecasting spreadsheet.
- While we don't know how much our investments will grow in the future, we need to plan on the basis of how assets have grown in the past.
- Based on a review of historic returns we can assume a well-balanced portfolio with at least 60% equity will grow at around 4-6% after inflation each year.
- When you start saving 'outweighs' how much you save because of the power of compounding. Starting saving early in life makes a huge difference.

10

BUDGETING

KEEPING YOUR FINANCES UNDER CONTROL

To be sure you can save and invest enough you need to manage your spending. To do that you need to budget in some way. Some people have the stamina to do this in full detail and budget and track every item of spending in a spreadsheet or on an app, but most of us don't have the patience for that and need something simpler we can stick to.

The simplest systems use 'pots' or 'buckets' of spend and each month money is designated into separate spend and save pots. Many follow the simple 50/30/20 rule, popularised by Elizabeth Warren, the US senator, in a book she wrote with her daughter in 2005[28]. The plan categorises spending into 3 buckets: Needs, wants and savings. 50% goes into needs such as rent/mortgage, insurance, utilities, groceries, commuting costs, essential clothing and any committed repayments (e.g., car payments). 30% goes into wants which is for all your spend on non-essentials such as dining out, coffees, holidays, concerts, non-essential clothes shopping, TV subscriptions, gym membership, gadgets and non-essential car upgrades. If you give regularly to charities, that could be in the needs or wants category, depending on how you see it. The third bucket, 20%, is for clearing (non-mortgage) debt, building up a rainy day fund and long-term investing; this bucket is sometimes referred to as 'future you'. Some advocate having separate bank accounts. Scott Pape, the Australian author and media personality, aka 'The Barefoot Investor', also advocates a bucket system, though a bit different to the 50/30/20 system. He goes so far as to advocate having different bank cards and giving the accounts nicknames like 'daily expenses', 'mojo' (rainy day account) and 'splurge'; some of his followers even write these nicknames on their cards to make sure they stick to the plan.

Either way, the savings need to come off the top automatically every month. Some talk about 'paying yourself first', with a regular amount going into your pension and ISA every month as soon as the pay cheque is in the account. Ideally you want to adopt a 'set and forget' approach to savings and set a regular standing/debit order to your ISA and a regular payroll deduction for your pension (or SIPP if you are self-employed), so the savings go out without you having to think about it or do anything.

The percentages may need to be different for you and vary depending on your situation. If you live in a high-cost housing area, you may need more than 50% for essentials. This is a rule of thumb, a benchmark; you need to work out what's right for you. But if you can't afford to save and invest, you need to make some changes; lower your spending and/or increase your income. It's about being in control of your finances and if you are always living from hand to mouth or yo-yoing in and out of overdraft or credit card debt, then you are not in control.

It's important to regularly check and haggle with your service providers to keep your everyday expenses low. Fortunately for the bashful, you don't have to do this in person as much but can use comparison sites and just dump the old supplier online. For the big costs, like utilities, you need to do this every year, as the savings can be considerable. If you would prefer to avoid the hassle of switching, once you have a new quote you should call your current supplier and tell them you are going to switch to save money, but would like to stay with them and ask them what they can do to make that possible. This works particularly well with broadband/media providers. Be firm and be clear you will leave if they don't come to the party. Chances are they will. Also, if you have a mortgage that is coming to the end of a discount window, make sure you have renegotiated and agreed on a mortgage deal with your existing lender or a new one. If you don't do this on time you will end up paying the much more expensive standard variable rate until this is sorted.

DEBT AND WHAT TO PAY OFF
BEFORE YOU START INVESTING

Should you be debt free before you start investing? And if you are not, is paying down debt not a better use of any spare cash than investing?

It depends on the type of debt.

CREDIT CARD DEBT

At all costs, avoid credit card debt. It's very expensive and you should not have to go into debt for the sorts of things a credit card buys. If you are going into debt for everyday consumption, clothes, holidays and/or gadgets you need to have a serious look at your budget and cut back. Famously in 2003, Matt Barrett, the then Chief Executive of Barclays, the owner of Barclaycard, told the Treasury Select Committee that he would not borrow money using a credit card because it was too expensive. He also revealed to the Committee that he had told his four adult children not to rack up debt on their cards either. If the Chief Executive of a company, which makes its money from credit card debt, tells you not to use it because it's too expensive, then it's a good idea to take his advice!

And the interest rates are very expensive. Average credit card interest rates are around 20%, with the highest rates currently close to 40%. It's surprising that these rates are allowed, but they are, so you need to make sure you never end up paying them.

Most people find it convenient to have a credit card. It provides some consumer protection, which can be especially useful when shopping online, it's useful when travelling (most car hire companies won't do business with you unless you have one) and you can earn points, airmiles or cashback. But you need to make sure you pay it in full every month. So set up a debit order, to give the credit card company the right to settle the full outstanding balance every month. If you don't do this, you would be better off cutting up the card and living without it, as you are going to end up paying very high rates of interest every month. If you are short of money one month, ask your bank for a loan or overdraft instead: the rate is bound to be much cheaper than your credit card. Pay it off as soon as you can.

Don't be taken in by zero-interest transfer deals. These are teaser rates and you are only being offered this rate because the company knows they are going to make money out of your high credit card debt at a later stage. Clearly, if you have got yourself into credit card debt, they can be a cheap way out of it, but only use this in that extreme situation on a one-off basis.

Also, don't get too excited by the points, airmiles or cashback. Even with the very best schemes, the value of these benefits is seldom more than 1% of spend and often it's closer to 0.25%. That's only £2.50 for every £1,000 of spend. And unless it's cashback, you actually have to use the points/airmiles. If it's airmiles you should be aware that it's often quite difficult to get rewards flights for the times you want to travel.

A quick explanation of the consumer protections you get with a credit card. Anything you buy with a credit card that costs between £100 and £30,000 is protected under Section 75 of the Consumer Credit Act. If the item is faulty or not delivered, you can claim back from the card provider. So if you buy a new bike online and the company goes bust before delivering it, you can claim from the credit card company. Or if you book car hire for your holiday and get there to find the agent hasn't paid the hire company, you can claim from the credit card company (yes, this one happened to me). You do get some protection from a debit card purchase under 'chargeback', a voluntary scheme that the major card issuers have signed up to, but it's much more limited than the credit card protections.

Credit cards don't charge interest from the day of purchase until the monthly account settlement date, so that window is interest free. However, generally this does not apply to cash withdrawals from your credit card, which incur interest from the day of withdrawal. So don't use your credit card to withdraw cash.

You also need to be sure you understand the charges for using your credit card abroad. Typically the costs of foreign currency is made up of two components (1) the 'spread' on the exchange rate and (2) the fee. The spread is best understood as the difference between the 'buy' and 'sell' rates of the currency.

If when buying Euro you get €1.13 for each pound, but to exchange Euro for pounds you are charged €1.14 for a pound, the spread is 1c. Usually for the larger currencies the spread is lower, whereas more exotic currencies have wider spreads. On top of that your credit card will charge a fee, usually 2–3%. Credit cards usually have a very low spread, compared with other forms of foreign exchange. The spread is set by the credit card networks e.g., Visa, Mastercard and doesn't vary between the banks issuing the card, but the fee does. If you can get a credit card that has a low or zero foreign currency fee, then do so. Also make sure you understand the ins and outs of how this fee applies to purchases and cash, as it may well be more costly to withdraw cash.

If you have credit card debt, sort this out. This has to be a priority over investing. You would be very lucky indeed to get 18 or 19% return on your investments, so the best use of any spare cash is to pay down this expensive debt as fast as you can.

Many advise against ever getting a credit card or those who have had difficulties managing their debt to cut up their cards and never get another one. For many people this is the right strategy; while there are benefits to having a credit card, you can easily live without one. The value of points or airmiles are actually a very small percentage of the spend and will quickly be wiped out if you ever need to use their very expensive credit. And it really simplifies your finances, as everything you spend has to be money you physically have in your bank account.

CAR FINANCING

In general, it is best to avoid debt to purchase a car, but there are circumstances where it may make sense to lease a vehicle and carry on investing. If you need a car for your work and run a high mileage, it may make sense to lease it. There are tax advantages to leasing a car if you are able to do so in connection with your work, and sometimes you can get relatively low effective interest rates on a lease. If the car is an electric vehicle, the 'Benefit in Kind' tax for private use is very low and you get some tax subsidy towards your costs.

However, a car is an expense and typically loses over half its value after three years of use. If you are simply buying a new car because you want to, you need to be clear you are consuming around 20% of its new price every year plus the cost of the interest. And these days a three-year-old car is still very reliable and won't cost you any more in maintenance than a new one, so from a pure economic utility perspective it makes sense to buy one a few years old. But if cars are your thing and a new car is important to you, and you can afford it and still have money available to invest what you need to, then you should do so. But if not, save up and buy a decent second-hand car without going into debt.

STUDENT 'DEBT'

Student debt in the UK isn't really debt, it's really a rather complicated graduate tax. With the current scheme, you pay back at a rate of 9% of your salary above £27,295 when you start working (the threshold increases each year with inflation). The interest rates are high, currently up to 5.4%; higher than you would pay on a mortgage. You only pay the highest interest if you earn more than £47,835. You pay interest at RPI (Retail Price Index[29]) until you earn above £27,295, and currently that's 2.4%. Then between £27,295 and £49,130 it rises from RPI to RPI + 3% on a sliding scale. But if you haven't paid it all off 30 years after leaving university, it's written off. It's estimated that over 80% of people will never pay off their student debt and will have it written off. Clearly if you are one of the 80% who are not going to ever earn enough to pay it off, you shouldn't.

But what if you are a very high earner, and you pay less on your mortgage, should you pay this off as a priority before investing? The answer is probably not. If you are absolutely certain that you will continue to earn at a high rate for the remainder of your 30 years since graduating, possibly. You need to be sure that you aren't going to throw it all in and downshift or work for a charity or take some time out to be a full-time parent or return to being a student. Remember your outstanding 'loan' doesn't feature in any credit score. If you are saving up for a deposit or want to stretch yourself to a larger property, the extra deposit from the additional investment will be more valuable than having settled your student loan.

MORTGAGE

Should you pay off your mortgage before investing? The short answer is no. Mortgage rates are very low, with many paying less than RPI on their mortgage. At those rates there is no hurry to pay it off, you should be able to get a better return over the long-term from your investment portfolio.

RAINY DAY CASH

How much ready cash should you have before investing? The often-quoted rule of thumb is a 'rainy day fund' of three months of spending. The idea is that if you lose your job, that will be enough to tide you over. But that really depends on your personal circumstances. How stable is your job? What sort of redundancy payout would you get? How variable are your expenses? If you are living with a partner could you manage on just one salary between the two of you? Are your investments in more liquid ISAs or locked away in a pension? Don't overthink it, it's a good thing to have some cash and three months of spending is a good benchmark. It's often advised that you put this in a separate account with a different bank to the one you use day to day, so you make it difficult to raid your rainy day fund without good reason.

We know that it is often said that money is the number one cause of stress and that most people experience money-related anxiety from time to time. For most, it's not the shortage of money that's the issue, it's that they don't have their finances under control. We know that beyond a basic level of income, money doesn't bring happiness. But adopting a simple set of rules to manage your money and forming habits to live by them, really will reduce your stress and help you live a happier life.

In summary:

- The simplest budgeting systems use 'pots' or 'buckets' of spend and each month money is designated into separate spend and save pots.
- Many follow the simple 50/30/20 rule of Needs/Wants/ Savings.
- Whatever system you use it is important to 'pay yourself first' with a regular amount automatically going into your pensions and ISA every month before all other spending.
- Paying down debt should often be a priority over investing, though some forms of debt, such as mortgage debt, are so cheap that you shouldn't delay investing until they are paid off.
- Credit card interest rates are very expensive and you should never have credit card debt.

- You should always settle your credit card every month with a debit order and if you don't have the discipline to control your spending, cut it up and live without it.
- In general, it is best to avoid debt to purchase a car, but if you need a car for work and do a high mileage it may sometimes be worth leasing, especially if it's an electric vehicle.
- Student debt in the UK isn't really debt, it's really a rather a complicated graduate tax.
- Generally, unless you are a very high earner and very sure your earnings will stay high for a long time, it doesn't make sense to pay off your student 'loan' early.
- It's a good idea to have a rainy day fund of around three months of spending, in a separate account, so you can manage unforeseen spend or loss of income without going into debt.
- For most of us financial stress is not about *not having enough*, but rather because we don't have our finances under control.
- Adopting a simple set of rules to manage your money and forming habits to live by them, really will reduce your stress and help you live a happier life.

11

INSURANCE AND PROTECTION

MANAGING YOUR NON-INVESTMENT RISKS

This is a book focused on investment and not a general personal finance book, but you do need to think about insurance alongside investments; after all, insurance is risk management.

The starting principle is only insure what you can't afford to lose. Insurance is expensive and it's almost always cheaper to self-insure. Don't buy the add-on insurance with the iPhone (unless you are particularly prone to losing things!) or the extended warranty they try and sell you when you buy a laptop or a new kitchen appliance.

HOME AND CAR INSURANCE

If you own a home, you need to insure it and the contents, if you own a car you need to insure it. You can shop around on comparison websites to get the best deal, or to check that your renewal rate is fair. Generally, loyalty is not rewarded; the business model is to price cheaply for new customers and claw that back from the customers who stay.

But you don't always have to actually move insurers; it often pays to haggle with your existing insurer. A few months back I got the renewal quote for our second car (the one used by a learner in the family) and the price was way too high. But I didn't really want to move insurer, it's a hassle and I was busy. So I did a quick check on a comparison site, then called the insurer and asked them to reconsider, said I could get it cheaper elsewhere, but wanted to stay with them. And they gave me a £250 discount there and then. What was most surprising is that they gave me a larger discount than I asked for!

TRAVEL INSURANCE

You need travel insurance if you are going abroad. A short hospital stay in the US could wipe you out. Needing to be repatriated from Europe could do the same. A friend had to be flown back from a holiday in Spain, because of complications in her pregnancy. They put her on a charter flight with a nurse attending and it cost over £100,000. Mother and baby were fine; and mother was very grateful she had the insurance. Shop around for travel insurance, and make sure you understand what you are getting; no point in paying for something that doesn't provide the cover you need. Many credit cards provide travel cover, providing you purchased the flight/holiday through them. But you need to read the fine print to check this covers what you need. And remember if you have any health issue, you need to declare this and you may need to pay a surcharge or purchase separate insurance; if you don't this could invalidate your insurance.

If you have ever rented a car on holiday, you will be familiar with the excess charges on car rental insurance. You could just run the risk and pay the excess if you have an accident, but I tend to insure for this – the excess can be quite high and I don't have much faith in car hire companies not slapping me with a spurious claim for a scratch that was there all along. But never buy the additional excess protection insurance they try and sell you at the counter. Normally the cheapest option is to buy this excess insurance separately ahead of the trip (online). I tend to hire a car a few times a year so find it cheaper to just buy an annual policy when I need one and then the first time I rent a car after that policy expires I buy another annual policy. If you are booking your car online with an aggregator site, you may find they offer a 'no excess' option and it's a good deal, or they offer add-on insurance that's a reasonable price.

While we are on car hire, I should add it's not just excess insurance you shouldn't buy at the counter: never buy any extras or upgrades they try and sell you at the counter. When you get there, you are tired from your journey, and if it is peak time, fed up with the queue, maybe you have kids who are tired and restless and you are at your weakest, and sometimes it's just easier to say yes, whatever. And they know that and take full advantage.

HEALTH AND DENTAL INSURANCE

In the UK we don't need health or dental insurance; we have the NHS. However, having health insurance will help you jump the queue and give you a better experience if you need in-patient care, but it's not essential. It's difficult to get an NHS dentist as an adult in the UK, so most people pay out of their own pocket, and dental insurance helps smooth the cost, but again it's not essential. If your company offers a scheme for health and/or dental insurance, and it is free, of course you take it; or if it's discounted at 'group rates', it may well be worth it for the peace of mind. Otherwise, it's a matter of deciding if this is important enough to you to be a priority.

LIFE ASSURANCE AND DISABILITY INSURANCE

If you have dependents and you don't have a big enough pot of savings and investments to pay off any debt and cover their needs were you to die, you need life cover. Similarly, you need cover to pay living expenses if you become disabled and could no longer work and support yourself and those who depend on you. If you're employed, your company may offer one or both of these either for free or at discounted 'group' rates. Bear in mind if you ever leave your current firm, you won't be covered, and may need to purchase this directly then. If meanwhile you have a health issue, this cover may be harder and/or more expensive to get, so it may be worth buying some protection independently. How much cover do you need? For life cover it's at least enough to pay off your mortgage and close the gap to the number you worked out in Chapter 9 (Investing Enough) – and it may well be more if you need to make provision for children. For disability cover, it will be more than this. This is one area where you may need advice: it's complicated and the consequences of getting it wrong could be catastrophic.

In summary:
- You need to think about insurance alongside investments; insurance is risk management.
- The starting principle should be to only insure what you can't afford to lose.
- You need home and car insurance; shop around and/or haggle to make sure you get a good deal.

- If you travel abroad, you need travel insurance; the cost of a short stay in a foreign hospital could wipe you out.
- Health and dental insurance are not essential in the UK, we have the NHS. But if the benefits of private insurance are important to you, then this needs to be factored into your spending priorities.
- If you have dependants and your investments, after paying off debt, are not enough to cover their needs were you to die, you need life assurance. Similarly, you may need disability cover. This is one area where you may need advice: it's complicated and the consequences of getting it wrong could be catastrophic.

12

"BUT I WANT TO HAVE SOME FUN WITH MY INVESTMENTS."

THE CORE-SATELLITE APPROACH

Some people like to have a bit of fun with their investments. They have a view on what's going to happen to particular stocks or industries and want to invest and reap the rewards when those views turn out to be right. Of course, rationally we know they are unlikely to be right more than half the time, but for some it's more important to play the odds.

If this is you then there are a few options. Firstly, you could set up a virtual investment portfolio and test how good you actually are, without it costing you anything when your picks don't turn out as you would like them to. There are apps that you can use to manage your virtual trades and track your performance. If you find that rewarding and decide to do this for real, then you need to be sure to keep this to a small percentage of your overall investment, i.e., 90% of your investments in a diversified ready-made portfolio and just 10% in your 'dabbling' portfolio. That way, if luck goes against you, you haven't put your whole portfolio at risk. Or putting it another way, you have maintained a well-diversified portfolio without your 'dabbling' portfolio destabilising the balance of the diversification and increasing the risk of loss.

This is a 'core-satellite' approach. The core of your portfolio is a well-diversified, low-cost index-based investment and the satellite has more active holdings, be they selective direct equities or specialist funds. It may be that the satellite helps diversify the overall portfolio by exposure to specialist assets that are not in the core, e.g., exposure to commercial property via REITs or to earlier stage companies via a VCT or AIM portfolio. Or it may just be that you have a view on particular companies or active fund managers from your own research and want to express that in your holdings. The key is to ensure that these satellite holdings are not concentrated; with the absolute maximum of 5% of your portfolio in any one holding and that in total they do not upset the balance of your overall portfolio.

If you want to trade 'meme stocks' from Redditt board recommendations, these trades should be in your satellite portfolio. If you have Bitcoin/crypto FOMO, these 'investments' should be in your satellite portfolio. Of course, you will probably lose less money if you avoid these trades completely, but the satellite is for fun, a space to be irrational!

I've put a note on cryptocurrencies in the appendix, for those who are interested in my view on this. In short any 'investment' in cryptocurrencies is high-risk speculation, with a very high probability of losing you money, and a quite small chance of making a massively outsized return.

INVESTMENT TRUSTS

Funds are either 'open-ended' or 'closed-ended'. An open-ended fund issues new shares every time it takes on new investor funds so is able to grow as more investors join. There are different types of open-ended funds. Within the UK, the two main types are 'unit trusts' and 'OEICs' (Open-ended Investment Companies). One is in law a 'trust' and the other a 'company', but practically this doesn't make much difference to the investor.

A closed-ended fund, often referred to as an 'investment trust', issues a set number of shares with a fixed pool of capital at the outset. Once a closed-ended fund or investment trust has been set up anyone who wants to buy into the fund needs to do so on the secondary market, i.e., buy their shares from another investor who already has them. So, shares in investment trusts trade at a discount or a premium to the underlying assets depending on demand (and how good a job investors think the manager is doing).

Ready-made funds are generally open-ended funds. This works well for well-diversified portfolios with underlying very tradable passive index funds or ETFs. However, with more specialist holdings if something happens to cause a large proportion of the investors to divest, the portfolio manager has to sell down rapidly to keep up with demand and this may not always be easy to do. The investment trust manager doesn't have this problem. The capital within the fund is unaffected by what happens in the secondary market. So, where the investment manager wants to buy investments that are 'illiquid', such as shares in private companies, not listed on a stock exchange, it often makes more sense to use an investment trust type structure. Even where this is not the case, some managers prefer the investment trust structure as it encourages a longer-term view. There are also some technical differences; for example, an investment trust can borrow to invest and are allowed to retain some of the earnings from investments, enabling some smoothing of income. Calling these funds 'trusts' is a bit of a misnomer, in that they are actually companies, listed on the stock exchange, and when you invest in an investment trust you become a shareholder of the company, just as you would be with any other equity.

While the price of an investment trust is set 'in the market' through trading supply and demand, an open-ended trust has its price set once each day, based on the market valuation of the underlying investments. Investment trusts' fees are generally a little lower than those of open-ended funds. And there has been analysis done that suggests their performance is superior over the long run vs other active funds (and this is likely to be at least partly because of their low fees), although the gearing allowed for these vehicles does lead to greater volatility in the short-term. Investment trusts have a small fan club in personal investment circles, no doubt partly because of the lower fees/higher performance. Because they trade in the market their price is technically independent of the value of the underlying holdings, and quite often they trade at a discount to the underlying value, giving an extra potential advantage to investors. They are well worth considering in your satellite portfolio if you want to try your hand at picking long-term active winners. And certainly less risky than buying individual shares.

HOW DOES PROPERTY FIT INTO MY PORTFOLIO?

Your own home is not really an investment. It is a place to live. The alternative is renting, so from a purely economic standpoint, we buy a house on the basis that over the long-term we will pay less in mortgage interest than rent.

I think it is a good idea to buy your own home if you can afford to do so. From time to time a personal finance journalist writes an article working out the long-term economics of rent vs buy. Mostly they conclude it is better to buy, though sometimes they conclude it's cheaper to rent. However, the key reason I think it's good to buy is it's a form of forced savings. Once you have the mortgage you will pay it off even if it takes 20 or 25 years. You will fix the house, and you will make improvements. Some of these will add value, others won't but at the end of the day you will have a paid-for house. The alternative is you rent and put some extra money away and build up a portfolio to the same value. But you probably won't. In the lean years you may stop investing or even have to withdraw some of your savings. That's more difficult to do if you have a mortgage – you have to keep paying it and it's quite difficult to sell bits of your house. Yes, you can remortgage, but it's a hassle and often hard to do if you're in a lean year.

However, don't overreach on borrowing. Build up a sensible deposit, at least 10% to 15% or more if you can. For many in the UK, that means waiting a long time before buying, but that's not necessarily a bad thing. We've had a few decades of extraordinary property price growth in the UK (and globally). This makes homes very expensive. Don't plan on prices going up at the same rate going forward. It's reasonable to assume that prices will grow in line with inflation going forward. Of course, we don't know what will happen and there could well be a fall in price. We do know that mortgage rates are very low, and low rates have contributed to property price inflation. And that there is little room for rates to move a lot lower to further fuel property price inflation.

There are other reasons to buy a home. You get to live in the place as long as you like without the threat of needing to move at the end of a lease. You can make changes to suit you and you may even like DIY. But you are always going to need to live somewhere, so you can't really live off the value of your house in retirement. You may be able to downsize in retirement or move from an expensive city to a cheaper location and release capital. However, this sort of plan should be thought through very carefully. Will you really want to downsize or move away when the time comes? After transaction costs, how much will you realistically be able to release?

When we talk about physical property investment, we mean property other than your home; buy-to-let or holiday let properties. Buy-to-let was very popular in the late 90s and early 2000s. Property price inflation was very high and interest rates were low by historical standards and the banks were keen to lend. The tax regime was also generous. Quite a few people built up portfolios of properties by remortgaging to buy additional properties as the prices went up. It's not so easy anymore, but that's not to say it's not possible to make a decent return. While the tax position is not as generous and most people don't expect prices to rise much in the short-term, mortgage rates are at historic lows, so buy-to-let in the right locations can still be profitable. With the rise of Airbnb and the popularity of staycations and a more generous tax regime than for buy-to-let, holiday lets have grown in popularity in recent years.

For buy-to-let mortgages you can no longer deduct mortgage expenses from your rental income to reduce your tax bill, but instead you receive a tax credit based on 20% of your mortgage payments. So, for higher-rate taxpayers this means you won't get all the tax back on your mortgage payments as the credit only refunds at the basic 20% rate.

However, for holiday lets, you can still enjoy the full mortgage deduction at the higher rate, making these properties relatively more attractive to some investors. Also, if you incorporate a company to own one or more buy-to-let properties, then the full mortgage interest deduction still applies. This is unlikely to be worth doing for a buy-to-let you already own, as you will have to pay Stamp Duty and may well have to pay Capital Gains Tax.

It's not in the scope of this book to go into the ins and outs of property investing in any detail. However, as with any investment, make sure you do your homework. Investing in property has risk and while borrowing (at current low rates) increases the yield, it also increases the risk. If the property is empty the mortgage still needs to be paid. People often underestimate the costs of maintaining and servicing a property, and property investment can be demanding timewise. Your ISA portfolio won't call you at 10pm at night to complain about a leaking toilet.

Investing in buy-to-let or holiday property is very different from investing in the capital markets. It requires time and attention, and physical property is a lot less liquid; when you need extra cash, it's going to take a lot more time to sell your property than it would an investment fund. One property, even with a mortgage, ties up a lot of capital. Lenders usually require at least a 25% deposit. That's quite a few eggs tied up in one basket.

The British have a bias towards property investing, and that's been reinforced by the massive gains some people have made on property in the last 25 years or so. Some seem to think property never goes down in value. You need to be wary of the 'true believers' in property investing, especially those making money from selling you investing courses. At the end of the day, it is just another asset class, with its pros and cons.

If you decide you do want to invest in physical property you need to think about how this fits in your overall investment portfolio, as investment property behaves differently to an equity or indeed a bond portfolio. Physical property prices do go up and down, but generally not to the same extent as equities, though prices can fall by quite a bit. In the early 1990's property crash, UK property prices declined by about 20%, though in London and the South East the reversal was around 35%: this was a time of very high interest rates and fire sales because people couldn't afford the mortgages. In the 2007/2008 crisis, the falls were much lower because rates came down and there were fewer mortgage holders in difficulty. Given that property prices behave differently to equities, investing in property can provide some diversity and balance in your portfolio and potentially reduce the effects of an equity downdraft.

PROPERTY FUNDS

Rather than holding physical property you can access the property market through an investment fund. Your ready-made investment may well have property funds or property indices as an investment, but if it doesn't you may want to hold some property in your satellite portfolio. For the most part, these funds invest in commercial properties, although increasingly they are investing in build-to-rent apartment block developments.

Should you decide at any point to invest in property funds directly, you should be aware of the practicalities of the two types of property fund. Like other investment funds, there are 'open-ended' funds and 'closed-ended' funds (also known as investment trusts).

Open-ended property funds allow new investors to invest capital into the fund and purchase units in the fund and also allow investors to sell units in the fund. But property is illiquid; it takes time to buy and/or sell property. So, these funds keep a cash reserve to ensure that they can fund unit redemptions without putting themselves in the position of having to sell under pressure. Unfortunately, this doesn't always work, and if there is a sudden downturn and investors want out, some funds find themselves in the position of not being able sell their properties fast enough to meet investors' demand for liquidity. They then have to 'gate' the fund; that is, close the fund to withdrawals for a time to give the fund managers time to sell more properties. Investors are then in the difficult position of holding financial assets they can't sell. Once the fund is gated, many of the remaining investors get nervous fuelling a vicious circle, often resulting in the fund being wound down. The FCA (the Financial Conduct Authority, the regulator) is concerned about this and is even considering making all open-ended property fund withdrawals subject to a six-month notice period.

Closed-ended funds or real estate investment trusts (REITs) don't allow investors to add new capital after the initial public offering. These funds have a fixed amount of capital and trade on a stock exchange. If investors want to redeem their investment, they can simply sell their shares in the trust through an exchange. The price of the REIT will be at a premium to the net asset value (NAV) of the underlying real estate investments if there is strong investor demand; and the REIT may well trade at a discount to the NAV when demand is weak. For the investor, it means you can always cash in your investment. Because of this ability to trade in and out via the stock exchange, over the short-term REITs display equity-like volatility, but over the long-term they are more closely aligned to the property market.

Arguably the closed-ended REIT is a more suitable fund structure for illiquid property assets than the open-ended fund. The fund manager only has one shot at raising capital with a REIT – at the IPO – so the attraction of the open-ended structure for the manager is clear. But as an investor, you should be fully aware of the liquidity risk of the open-ended property fund before you commit your capital.

In summary:

Core satellite
- Some people like to have a bit of fun with their investments and take a view on particular shares or sectors and reap the reward when they turn out to be right.
- Of course, rationally we know they are unlikely to be right more than half the time, but for some it's more important to play the odds.
- If this is you then it's best to adopt a core-satellite approach, with the core of your portfolio in a well-diversified fund, and with the satellite of your 'dabbling' investments making up no more than 10% of your overall holdings.
- Investment trusts are well worth considering if you are looking to add active funds to your satellite portfolio. They are long-term oriented, have low fees and some studies have shown that they generally outperform.

Property investing
- It is generally a good idea to buy your own home if you can afford to; it's a form of disciplined saving and at the

end of 20–25 years you will have a paid-off house. But your house is not really an investment asset, it's a place to live.

- Given that property prices behave differently to equities, investing in property can provide some diversity and balance and potentially reduce the effects of an equity downdraft.

- Buy-to-lets or holiday lets are ways of building up property investment assets. Recent changes to the tax regime for buy-to-let make it less attractive than it was, however mortgage rates are at historic lows and it's still possible to make a good return.

- The tax regime for holiday lets is more attractive, and with the rise of Airbnb and the increasing popularity of 'staycations', holiday lets have grown in popularity.

- The British have a bias towards property investing, and you need to do your sums carefully for each investment to ensure you fully understand the actual return and the risk.

- Rather than hold physical property you can invest in a property fund. There are two broad types of property fund: open-ended and closed-ended (also known as real estate investment trusts (REITS)). Arguably the REIT structure is more suitable for illiquid property assets than an open-ended fund.

13

PERFORMANCE

IS MY PORTFOLIO BEHAVING AS I EXPECT IT TO?

Fund promotional materials all have a disclaimer to the effect that "*past performance may not be an indicator of future results*". And, of course, we know that while the statement is true, very few of us will ignore past performance in assessing an investment. And rightly so. If a fund has been a poor performer over multiple years, you need a very good reason to invest in the promise it will do better going forward. Equally, it's difficult to separate skill from luck when assessing historic outperformance and generally performance 'reverts to the mean'. So, we need to be wary of thinking a high-performing fund will keep doing so going forward. And most active portfolios won't outperform passive portfolios over time.

Remember that passive portfolios are not truly passive. The fund manager is making asset allocation choices and there will be differences in performance because of this. For example, if a passive portfolio is more heavily US market weighted in a good year for US equities, then that portfolio will outperform another portfolio with a more even allocation across developed markets. But between well-diversified passive portfolios these variations shouldn't be large.

So, before we buy a diversified fund or a robo-portfolio, most of us will want to see how it has performed in the past so we can check it's in line with our expectations of performance we have set in our plans. Once we own the fund or portfolio, we will want to check we are on track. We are also interested in how the performance was achieved from a risk perspective. If we get a high return on our portfolio, we want to also know its volatility. For example, if we have invested in a moderate-risk balanced equity/bond portfolio we don't want superior performance at the cost of taking on more risk than we have bought into.

With this in mind, let's look at some analysis of risk and performance of some typical funds. For all of this analysis I have used the three years to end of March 2022. Fund performance should be viewed over a reasonable term, hence the three years. Of course, this three-year window includes the global pandemic of the first half of 2020, which suppressed the performance of most diverse funds. Generally, by the end of March 2022, most funds will have recovered the losses incurred in the early stages of the pandemic.

For the first chart I have shown the performance vs risk (volatility) for three multi-asset fund ranges. The first two are from Quilter Investors, one of the larger providers of multi-asset funds to the private client industry with around £20bn of investor assets. You may not have heard of them as they mostly distribute through advisors, but you can buy their funds from the major platforms. The fund ranges are the Cirilium (Active) Portfolios and the Cirilium Passive Portfolios. Each range

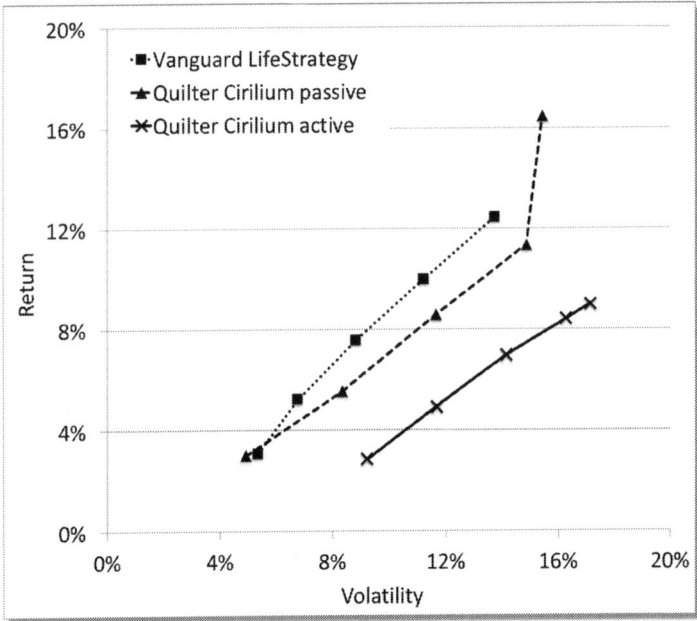

Figure 8: *Active and passive fund performance vs risk*

comprises five risk-profiled funds ranging from 'Conservative' to 'Adventurous'. I have chosen these two funds because they both have passive and active ranges.

In Figure 8, I have shown the performance vs risk for the active and passive ranges of Quilter and I have also shown the Vanguard LifeStrategy fund range. Unfortunately, I cannot show the Blackrock MyMap fund range as it's too new to have a three-year performance record. The LifeStrategy range behaves as we would expect, with each profile stepping up in risk and performance as the equity weighting increases. Also, the Quilter passive range has outperformed the active range. I am not sure why the highest-risk Quilter passive has such a high performance over this window, but it must be explained by

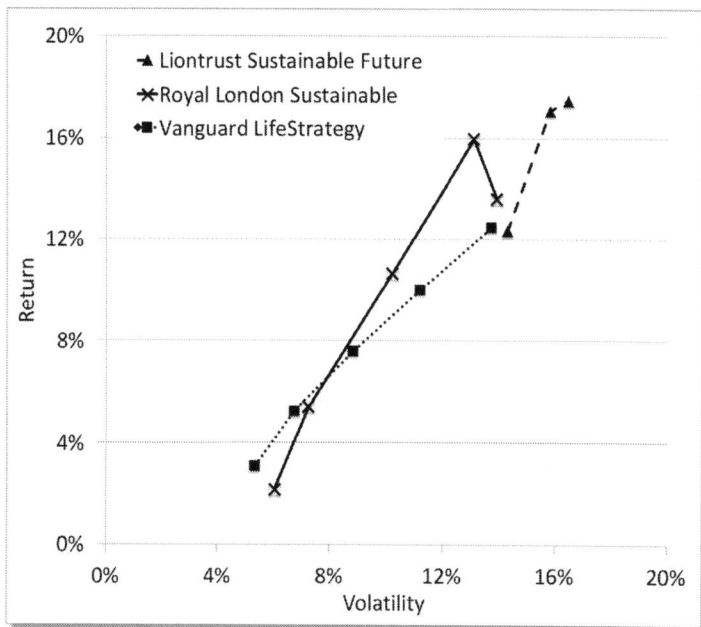

Figure 9: ESG fund performance

their asset allocation; also note the higher volatility of this fund than the other passives.

For the next chart I have shown the performance of the two (active) ESG fund ranges we discussed in Chapter 8; the Liontrust Sustainable Future range and the globally diversified funds in Royal London Sustainable range. Again, I have included the Vanguard LifeStrategy range as a comparator. You will see that, with the exception of the more conservative funds both ranges outperform the Vanguard LifeStrategy Funds over this window. For Liontrust, we can see that its higher equity funds have taken on more risk, given the volatility of two of the funds is higher than that of the 100%-equity Vanguard fund. The remaining explanation must be from underlying active manager performance and asset allocation. We know that ESG funds by definition have avoided some sectors that have not done well in this period (e.g., oil and gas) and have a higher allocation to sectors that have done well (e.g. tech and pharma), so this may well be part of the explanation.

So, what should you conclude from this? Some of you may conclude that you should buy one of the Liontrust or Royal London portfolios because of their superior performance over the last 3 years. If so, remember the disclaimer that *"past performance may not be an indicator of future results"*. Personally, I don't think any of this should change your thinking on choosing a fund; rather, I hope it has helped you make sense of some of the theory we discussed in early chapters. You should now see, practically, how a series of risk-profiled funds behave over a particular three-year window. This is a relatively short period, and one that included a global pandemic of unprecedented human impact.

In summary:

- While we are warned that *"past performance may not be an indicator of future results"*, we will want to review past performance when assessing an investment.
- In doing so we also need to assess the risk taken on by the fund, through its volatility, to be sure, for example, that outperformance has not been at the cost of taking on more risk than we have bought into.
- Fund performance should be viewed over a reasonable length of time, i.e. three years. Investing is for the long haul.

14

STICKING WITH IT

AND HOW UNDERSTANDING BEHAVIOURAL FINANCE WILL HELP YOU

I often think the main reason investors need an advisor is to help them stick with the plan. Investors get nervous when the markets are volatile, they sell out after the markets have lost a bit and then don't know when to buy back in and end up losing out. If they have an advisor they trust, they have someone who can try and talk them out of this behaviour. If they don't have an advisor, they are going to need to be self-disciplined. This is referred to as investing with 'composure'. The analysis shows that the best approach is to ignore the short-term swings and invest for the long-term horizon. Those who stay invested for the long-term are likely to be rewarded for their patience.

One of the key challenges for investors is the temptation of 'market timing'. When markets are crashing, fear takes over and investors sell out. As a result, they miss out on the 'best' days, when the market turns, and this can be very costly. JP Morgan Asset Management estimated that if you missed just the 10 best days in the market over the 20 years, from January 1999 to December 2018, you would have lost well over half the upside from investing in the S&P 500. The returns for staying in the market were 5.62% annualised, dropping to 2.01% when missing the best 10 days[30]. They also point out that 6 of those 10 best days were within 2 weeks of the 10 worst days. The very best days in the market are often when it's at its most turbulent. To quote Terry Smith, the Chief Executive behind the very successful 'Fundsmith' business: "*When it comes to so-called market timing there are only two sorts of people: those who can't do it, and those who know they can't do it. It's safer and more profitable to be in the latter camp*"[31]. There's a twee, but true, saying that advisors are very fond of: "*It's **time** in the markets, not **timing** the markets that counts*".

Carl Richards, author of *The Behavior Gap* and who we met in the introduction, talks about the difference between investment returns (the returns achievable from your chosen investments) and investor returns (what you actually end up achieving) and the difference being the 'behaviour gap'. Every year Dalbar, the independent investment research firm, publishes its *Quantitative Analysis of Investor Behavior* report (QAIB)[32]. The 2020 report showed that the average equity fund investor in the US has achieved 5.96% annualised average returns – a pretty good outcome. However, if they had stayed invested in the S&P index that entire period, they would have made an average of 7.43% and if they had stayed invested in a global equity portfolio, they would have made 8.29%[33]. Perhaps these differences don't sound that large to you but putting it in $ numbers starting with $100,000 in January 2001, the average investor's pot would have grown to $318,000 by the end of 2020, the S&P 500 investment to $420,000 and the global equity investment to $492,000. To quote from the Dalbar research report:

"...the set of longer-term data analysed in these QAIB reports clearly show that people are more often than not their own worst enemies when it comes to investing. Often succumbing to short-term strategies such as market timing or performance chasing, many investors show a lack of knowledge and/or ability to exercise the necessary discipline to capture the benefits markets can provide over longer time horizons. In short, they too frequently wind up reacting to market maturations and lowering their longer-term returns".

We know that greed and fear can lead to poor investment decisions and if people play to more 'composed' versions of themselves they will make wiser investment decisions. While we've understood these concepts a long time, there has been much more talk and examination of human behaviour in decision-making in recent years with the popularisation of the field of 'behavioural economics'. Classical economic theory uses a concept of the 'economic man' ('homo economicus'), an idealised person who acts rationally, and with perfect knowledge, and who seeks to maximise personal utility of satisfaction. Behavioural economics tells us that there is a wide array of psychological factors that determine the behaviour of investors and we sometimes find it very hard to act rationally in a given situation. If we have a better understanding of how we behave we can work hard to avoid these pitfalls and make better decisions.

Daniel Kahneman, the Nobel-prize-winning economist/psychologist, identified that people regularly make irrational choices, even when they have pretty good information. He refers to two systems of thinking: System 1, 'intuition', in which we respond to the world in ways that we're not conscious of, that we don't control and System 2, 'reasoning', the mind's slower, analytical mode, controlled and effortful.

System 1 thinking is fast, effortless and often emotionally charged; it's also governed by habit, so it's difficult either to modify or to control. It's also how we think 98% of the time.

Of course, we couldn't survive without System 1 thinking; we learn to walk, it becomes a habit and we stop thinking about it. And through life we learn more habits, and how to assess people and situations without deep thought and analysis. But Kahneman discovered that we are far less rational and far less correct in our System 1 thinking than we believe we are. We all suffer from cognitive biases. And for our investments it's good that we understand some of the key biases, to protect ourselves from our own worst behaviours. To mention just a few:

Overconfidence: research has shown time and again that people are generally unrealistically optimistic and overconfident. Richard Thaler, another Nobel-prize-winning behavioural economist, writes of an experiment he conducts with his MBA class in Chicago[34]. He asks each student to estimate how well they will do in the course by decile. Students can pick the top 10%, or second 10% and so on. These are well-educated, numerate students; they wouldn't have got into a top business school otherwise. Typically less than 5% of the class expects their performance to be in the bottom half, and more than half the class expects to perform in the top 20%. And it's not just MBA students who are overconfident. The vast majority of people think their driving ability is above average, when clearly that's not the case for half of all drivers. Overconfident investors may believe they can time the market, even when decades of academic research have shown that we can't. Or they may overestimate their ability to identify winning investments.

So, if you hear how your friend has made a fortune with his stock-picking prowess, smile knowingly internally (you don't want to annoy him), and stick with your sensible well-diversified investment plan.

Loss aversion: people hate losses, and behavioural economists have found that losing something makes us twice as miserable as gaining the same thing makes us happy. When markets are going down (bear markets), loss aversion could cause us to sell out if we think markets are going to keep sliding and we then won't buy back in until the fear has passed, by which time the market is well above where we sold out. Kahneman argues that every peek at the performance of your portfolio is an opportunity for distress because you're more likely to be upset by losses than pleased by your gains.

The challenge with selling out ahead of a market dip is you have to time both the sell and the buy just right. I was chatting with a friend near the start of the Covid-19 crisis and he told me he sold out much of his equity portfolio just before the worst of the dip. He was very pleased with himself. A year or so later he mentioned he hadn't yet bought back in, he's never been quite sure when the timing was right. Unfortunately for him, the markets have recovered while he's been on the sidelines and he's now having to pay much more to buy back the same portfolio than he sold it for.

So, look at your portfolio just a few times a year to make sure everything is as it should be and any regular investments are getting invested, but don't look at it too often. And if you've lost some money because the market is down, take a deep breath, close your laptop and step away. I like the convenience of having my investment platform app on my phone, but there is a good argument for deleting it and only being able to see what's happening when I take the trouble to log on via my computer...

Status quo bias: for lots of reasons, people tend to stick with their current situation. At universities, students tend to sit in the same seats, even though they are free to move about. Of course, there is little material advantage to moving seats in a class, but people display the same bias when the stakes are much larger. Governments are more and more recognising the benefits of exploiting this bias to 'nudge' citizens into doing things they should do, as a cheap or costless way of delivering social policy. Pension auto-enrolment, which we explained earlier, was very deliberately brought in by David Cameron's coalition government to take advantage of the inertia bias. Most people stay with the default of investing in a pension, which reduces, in the long-term, the burden on the government providing a safety net for those who haven't saved enough for retirement. Unfortunately, those same investors are likely to stay in their retirement plan's default fund, which is likely to have too conservative an asset allocation to be suitable for a twenty-something new joiner.

So make sure you don't stick with the defaults, but review where you are invested in your company pension plan and take on the risk you should to meet your investing goals.

Regular monthly investing by a standing order or direct debit is a way of leveraging your status quo bias. If it's a tight month, or the markets are looking bearish, the money will carry on dripping in. The other advantage of regular investing is 'pound cost averaging'. By buying a fixed monetary amount of an investment each month you will buy into the ups and downs of the price of that investment and minimise the risk of buying at the top of the market.

You need to build a plan that works for you and compensates for your own foibles. I once worked with someone who set his watch fast so that he didn't miss his train. That wouldn't work for me, as I would know that I have the extra few minutes and adjust mentally, but somehow it worked for him.

They say habits are a way to avoid the exhaustion of having to regularly exercise self-control. If we get into a routine of doing something, it becomes a given in our day and we can stop thinking about whether we want to do it or not. We need to build saving and investing into a habit, to be sure we keep at it.

In summary:

- Investors need to build 'composure' – the ability to stay in the market for the long-term and ignore short-term swings.
- Avoid the temptation to try and time the market; generally, investors who try to do this miss the best days in the market and this can be very costly.
- Behavioural economics tells us that there is a wide array of psychological factors that determine the behaviour of investors and we sometimes find it hard to act rationally.
- This includes the risk that we are overconfident, loss-averse and biased towards the status quo.
- You need to build a plan that works for you and compensates for your own foibles; and build habits that protect you from your own irrational investing behaviour.

CONCLUSION

If you are reading this because you are one of those good people who only read a book in one direction and have now read everything else, thank you and well done!

So now all there is to do is to get on with it. In this book I have focused on demystifying investing and giving you the practical detail you need to do this yourself. You now have the tools to put together a plan to save and invest enough and to put that plan into action.

By using a ready-made low-cost fund, once you have set up a regular investing plan you don't need to spend lots of time tinkering with your portfolio. You just need to ensure you keep investing and stick with your plan through good markets and bad. Keep things simple and set up a standing order or direct debit to make monthly investments into your investments account each month and make sure you have set up your platform so your cash is invested each month. Once this is on autopilot you don't need to think about it, it just happens and in a few short years you will be pleased with the progress you have made.

As poets, philosophers and songwriters tell us, money can't buy happiness, but for so many people there is stress around their finances that makes them unhappy. And having a plan, and making it happen so you are in control of your finances, will make you happy.

APPENDIX 1

TAX – A BRIEF OVERVIEW

It's important for an investor to understand the effect of tax on their investments. We all know the government needs us to pay tax and most of us want to pull our weight and pay our fair share. But equally the tax system has been designed to encourage us to save and invest, so we don't become a burden on the state, and there is a place for sensible tax planning.

The four main taxes investors need to understand are:

- Income tax – paid on salary, rental income, interest, dividends, royalties.
- Capital gains tax (CGT) – paid on gains when you sell an asset during your lifetime.
- Inheritance tax – paid on your estate at death.
- Stamp duty/stamp duty land tax (SDLT) – paid on most share transactions and on real estate transactions.

How you invest can make a difference to the tax you pay, and you can use the tax saved to boost the amount you invest.

Income tax is generally taxed as follows (w.e.f 6 April 2022):

Band	Taxable Income	Tax rate
Personal allowance	Up to £12,570	0%
Basic rate	£12,571 to £50,270	20%
Higher rate	£50,271 to £150,000	40%
Additional rate	Over £150,000	45%

In addition, your employer will deduct National Insurance (NI) at 13.25% for income between £12,571pa and £50,270pa and at 3.25% for any income above £50,270. So, actually, the basic tax rate is 33.25% and the higher rate 43.25% and the highest additional rate is 48.25%. (Note the NI insurance rates for the self-employed are complex, but generally lower, so these rates will be different if you are self-employed.)

Income tax on dividends is at a slightly lower rate than that for other income, but the first £2,000 of income is free of tax.

If your investments are in an ISA or a pension you pay no tax on any income or gains while they are in these wrappers.

But the real leverage is the tax and NI savings from additional contributions into your pension. As an employee at the basic rate, every extra £100 you put into your pension costs you just £66.75 in take-home pay if you contribute by way of 'salary sacrifice' (£100 – £33.25 of tax & NI at 33.25%), and if you are at the higher rate that £100 will only cost you £56.75 in take-home pay. You will pay tax when you withdraw income from your pension when you retire, but 25% is tax-free (usually taken as a lump sum), your tax rate may well be lower and you won't be paying NI.

Savings into an ISA are out of post-tax income, but you won't pay any tax while it's within the ISA and you don't pay any tax when you withdraw money from your ISA. If you build up a significant ISA by the time you retire, you can fund a proportion of your retirement income from ISA drawdown and that income will be tax-free.

Capital gains tax (CGT) is charged at 10% for basic-rate taxpayers and 20% for higher- and additional-rate taxpayers, except for gains from residential property, where the rates are 18% and 28% (gains from selling your primary residence are free from CGT). The first £12,300 of gains is free of CGT. This is per individual, so if you own a second property jointly with your partner, then you can each claim this allowance on your share.

If you have a portfolio of investments outside of an ISA, you will pay tax on capital gains should you make gains over the £12,300 annual allowance, and also on dividend income, should that exceed the £2,000 tax-free allowance for dividends. You can reduce your exposure to future CGT by using the annual tax-free amount to 'harvest' gains in your portfolio. You can also sell loss-making funds/shares and offset losses against gains. Best to ensure all of your investments are within an ISA or a pension; that way you don't need to worry about paying this tax.

Also be aware that the 'personal savings allowance' means the first £1,000 of interest income is tax-free (£500 for higher-rate taxpayers). Given the very low interest rates paid on most accounts now, few investors will have enough cash to pay tax on interest.

As a married couple where one has a lower tax bracket, or pays no tax as they are out of the workplace, there is an opportunity to save tax by moving assets between spouses. All cash earning interest (above the tax-free amount) should be moved to an account in the name of the lower-taxed/non-tax-paying spouse. A similar approach can be taken if purchasing an investment property (though you need to be aware that if moving an existing property that has a mortgage, there may be stamp duty payable on the transfer, so be sure to take advice).

Another little known earner is the opportunity to pay into a pension for a non-earning partner. An individual can contribute up to £2,880 per year and receive basic-rate tax relief into a pension on the contribution, so a gross £3,600 into the pension. That's £720 per year free money.

Given pension and ISA savings allowances totalling £60,000 per year per individual, few people should need to invest outside of these tax shelters and end up paying tax on their investments pre-retirement. However, for those high earners who are able to save beyond these limits (or are capped out on pension allowances), then there is one other option that could be considered and that is to invest through one of the tax-efficient investment schemes designed to help small companies raise capital. There are three schemes: Enterprise Investment Scheme (EIS), Seed Enterprise Investments Scheme (SEIS) and Venture Capital Trusts (VCTs). There are a range of tax reliefs from these schemes, but the main one is income tax relief equal to 30% of the sum invested (50% SEIS). Given these are investments in smaller, early stage or less mature companies, these are higher risk investments and should be treated with caution. Furthermore, there are conditions tied to the tax reliefs that need to be clearly understood and it's recommended that you get specific financial planning advice before investing.

Inheritance tax is 40% on assets above £325,000 and a further £175,000 where a home is owned of at least that value. So, an individual who owns a property can leave £500,000 tax-free and a couple can leave £1m. There are further reductions for legacies left to charities. Surprisingly, any unused portion of a pension pot does not form part of an estate. It generally passes tax-free where the pensioner was under 75. Where he or she was over 75, the person inheriting will pay tax at their marginal income tax rate. The rules have some complexities and exceptions.

Inheritance tax is complicated and beyond the scope of this book to discuss in any detail. There are ways to minimise the inheritance tax bill; often the most effective one being to give away the assets before death. Where the donor survives 7 years after the gift, no tax is payable, with some 'taper' relief where the donor survives between 3 and 7 years. Setting up a trust is really a way of giving away assets while ensuring there is some oversight. But trusts have become less tax efficient, expensive and complex and are no longer suitable for many family situations. Some type of investment are exempt from inheritance tax, for example, a portfolio of qualifying AIM shares. AIM, stands for the 'Alternative Investment Market' and is the stock exchange for smaller, newer companies and as such AIM shares are generally a higher-risk investment. There are firms that specialise in managing AIM portfolios for this purpose.

Not much to say on stamp duty. It applies to most share transactions at 0.5% and to property transactions Stamp Duty Land Tax (SDLT) applies on a sliding scale as below:

Transfer value	SDLT
Up to £125,000	0%
The next £125,000 (from £125,001 to £250,000)	2%
The next £675,000 (from £250,001 to £925,000)	5%
The next £575,000 (from £925,001 to £1.5 million)	10%
The remaining amount (above £1.5 million)	12%

There is a discount for first-time buyers on properties up to £500,000 with no tax up to £300,000 and 5% on the portion over £300,000. If you already own a home and it's a second (or subsequent) home, then you pay an extra 3% SDLT on the whole purchase price.

In general, investors are allowed to arrange their affairs to minimise their tax. However, HMRC takes a dim view of aggressive avoidance and using loopholes to minimise tax. Of course, you should take advantage of the tax efficiency of pensions, ISAs and even enterprise investment schemes/VCTs (where properly managed) – the government is encouraging these investments for a good reason. But avoid anything that looks too good or too clever. And if you have a particular tax planning issue, make sure you get proper professional advice.

In summary:
- Income tax is paid on salary, rental income, interest, dividends and royalties.
- Capital gains tax (CGT) is paid on gains when you sell an asset in your lifetime. Importantly, the home you live in is exempt from CGT.
- If your investments are inside an ISA or a pension you don't pay income tax or CGT while the investment is inside the wrapper.
- Pension investments are from pre-tax income, and you can save tax by investing more into your pension (subject to annual and lifetime allowances). You pay tax when you eventually withdraw funds, but the first 25% is tax-free.
- ISA investments are from after-tax income, but you pay no tax when you withdraw.

- Inheritance tax is paid on your estate at death. Often the most effective way to save this tax is to give away assets before death.
- Stamp duty is paid on most share transactions and on real estate transactions.
- In general, taxpayers are allowed to arrange their affairs to minimise tax, however HMRC takes a dim view of aggressive avoidance and using loopholes. So, avoid any tax planning that looks too good or too clever.

APPENDIX 2

COMPANY SHARE PLANS

I have put this section in an appendix, because most people won't be working for employers who offer these schemes. However, if your employer does, you need to know about it as it's a great way to boost your savings and investments. The title for this section could also be, *How my Daughter Arranged a 5% Salary Raise After Just Six Months in her New Graduate Job*. All true. Yes, her employer has one of these schemes, and once she was through probation she could take it up and enjoy their generous matching payments into a share savings account.

The government wants to encourage employees to share in the ownership of companies they work for, and so provides tax incentives to make that happen. There are a number of incentives, but I will speak to just the two most popular types of share savings schemes for larger companies that are supported by HMRC: Save As You Earn (SAYE) and Share Incentive Plans (SIPs).

SAVE AS YOU EARN (SAYE)

This is a savings-related share scheme where you save for a 3- or 5-year window and then buy shares with your savings for a fixed price that is set at the beginning of the plan. You can save up to £500 a month under the scheme, though your company may set a lower limit.

The interest and any bonus at the end of the scheme is tax-free and you don't pay income tax or national insurance on the difference between what you pay for the shares and what they're worth.

SHARE INCENTIVE PLANS (SIPS)

In this plan you buy shares every month and your employer matches these share purchases by up to 2:1. Each employer sets its own limits and matching policy. The share purchase comes out of pre-tax income, though there is a limit to how much you can spend each tax year – the lower of either 10% of your income or £1,800.

You also get to buy more shares with any dividends you get. You need to keep the shares in the plan for up to 3 years to avoid paying income tax or national insurance on the value of the shares.

APPENDIX 3

CRYPTOCURRENCIES AS INVESTMENTS

Cryptocurrencies (cryptos), such as Bitcoin, are at best highly speculative investments. I am not saying you shouldn't put any money into Bitcoin or another one of the cryptos out there, but if you do you need to be honest with yourself about what you are doing and understand the risks. It's possible that the price of a particular crypto is supported by fundamentals, but it's overwhelmingly more likely that the cryptos price growth is driven by the 'greater fool theory'[35]. The greater fool theory says that you can make money from buying an overvalued investment (i.e., where the price is *not* supported by fundamentals), because there will be a 'greater fool' willing to pay you an even higher price when you sell. Or to put it another way, everyone's FOMO keeps driving the price up. Eventually the market runs out of 'greater fools' and the price collapses. The argument for fundamentals is that the underlying technology of a currency with a distributed ledger is valuable and that the particular crypto you are buying has some advantage in its deployment and/or technology and will be one of the winners when there is mass adoption of crypto into our day-to-day lives. That's possible, but most likely at some point a huge number of cryptos will cease trading and a lot of money will be lost.

You can think of cryptos as being most similar to commodities in their theoretical economic construct. Each currency is set up so there is a limited supply and with the hope that demand will grow, thus making each unit more valuable over time. The core concept of cryptos (i.e., a currency with a distributed ledger) is useful and valuable – and widespread adoption could make early investors in the successful players a very healthy return. While for many the main draw of cryptos is that they exist outside of the government and regulatory controls of traditional currencies, the harsh reality is that these currencies only exist because the regulators let them. The currencies that are willing and able to adapt to the constraints that the major regulators impose on them will end up being more successful than those that don't.

For regulators, the key concern is that crypto isn't used to launder money or finance terrorism; and they also worry that consumers could get caught up in scams and/or be defrauded. While until now the regulators oversight of cryptos has been very light, it won't stay that way. And when the regulators move there will be some currencies that won't be viable anymore and the costs for others will go up. The sheer number of cryptos in issue must be a concern for the regulators. At the time of writing there are said to be over 10,000 cryptos in issue. It's implausible that there is a viable market for any more than a small fraction of these currencies in the medium-term. For Bitcoin (the oldest and most popular of the cryptos) the environmental costs could end up being a constraint to its success, with environmentally responsible investors shunning it because of its heavy energy consumption and/or regulators moving against it (as China has already done). There's even the suggestion that governments could get in on the act, issuing cryptos of their own and potentially killing the market for the commercial players.

While for any investment you make, you need to be prepared to lose money, the risk with cryptos is of a different order of magnitude, with a very real possibility that you could lose most or all of your investment. Buying cryptos is pure speculation, with every investment having a small chance of paying off spectacularly, but a much greater chance of losing you all your money. Very few traditional asset managers will consider including cryptos in their client's portfolios, even in very small amounts. It is simply too difficult to make an objective investment case for investing clients' money in this market. If you feel you have an edge and can make a call as to the winning players then go ahead, but keep the amounts you invest small, because there is a very high chance that you will be proved wrong!

APPENDIX 4

SOME USEFUL WEBSITES/ BLOGS

Youngmoneyblog.co.uk

Founded by Iona Bain and targeted at the Millennial/Gen Z audience with a mission to ensure young people are financially knowledgeable, confident and in control of their futures. She has written a book (*Own It!*) and also hosts a podcast with the same name.

Finimize.com

With a *"…mission to empower everyone to become their own financial advisor. Providing the information and tools you need to invest with confidence"*. They have a five-minute daily financial news update, written for a younger audience in an easy-to-understand style. Also, events and an app. My caution is they have a lot of crypto and active content, most of which would be best ignored.

Boringmoney.co.uk

Founded by Holly Mackay, who has worked in the investment industry for two decades, *Boring Money* was set up to help normal people who don't have PhDs in finance make smart investment decisions quickly and painlessly. A great source of info on a full range of topics on the basics of investing and independent reviews on the providers. Also has a weekly newsletter/blog.

Pensioncraft.com

Set up by former investment banking investment strategist Ramin Nakisa. His blog has some very useful articles and educational videos on topics valuable to the novice DIY investor, including one on Blackrock MyMap vs Vanguard LifeStrategy and a few on active vs passive.

Morningstar.co.uk

A great source of free research on funds, and also a great source of news and views on the market and the fund industry.

Trustnet.com

Another great source of free research on funds, and also a great source of news and views on the market and the fund industry.

APPENDIX 5

FURTHER READING

If you want to read more, here are some options:

UK BOOKS

The Financial Times Guide to Saving and Investing for Retirement – the Definitive Handbook to Securing your Financial Future by Yoram Lustig (Pearson Education Limited, 2016): This book covers the full range of relevant topics for the UK DIY investor in an intelligent, thoughtful and structured way. The author is a professional asset manager, and he goes deeper into investment theory than most authors of DIY investment books while still keeping the content accessible to those outside of his profession.

The Financial Times Guide to Wealth Management – How to Plan, Invest and Protect Your Financial Assets by Jason Butler (Pearson Education Limited, 2nd edition, 2015): Jason Butler is a former financial planner, now 'financial well-being' expert, blogger, FT columnist and speaker. This guide covers the full range of topics for the investor, but with a stronger slant towards financial planning and holistic financial wellbeing. A good reference book for all 'wealth management' matters.

Own it! How Our Generation Can Invest Our Way to a Better Future by Iona Bain (Harriman House, 2021): Iona Bain is the founder of Young Money, a website about young people's finances https://www.youngmoneyblog.co.uk/, and considered to be one of the UK's leading millennial money experts. The book explains why you should invest and talks the reader through the range of options for investing at a high level. It has some very useful cautionaries on some of the popular, but potentially dangerous, investing fads.

***The DIY Investor* by Andy Bell** (Harriman House Limited, 3rd edition, 2021): Andy Bell is the founder of AJ Bell which he has grown into one of the largest investment platforms in the UK. This book covers the key topics for the DIY UK investor and explains to the reader how to build an investment portfolio in a low-cost tax-efficient way. In particular, he covers how to take advantage of the ISAs and SIPP tax wrappers and explains how to choose an investment platform. However, given the nature of his own business, he is perhaps constrained from being critical of the track record of the active fund management industry.

ON PASSIVE INVESTING

***The Little Book of Common Sense Investing* by John (Jack) Bogle** (John Wiley & Sons, 10th edition, 2017): Jack Bogle, the founder of Vanguard, is something of a cult figure in the world of index, or passive, investing. There is a collection of websites, blogs and chatrooms of dedicated 'Bogleheads', all committed to a better understanding and articulation of Jack Bogle's investment philosophy. This book outlines his philosophy in a simple and easy-to-read way. It was first written in 2010 and is the last one of his books to be updated by the author himself before he died in 2019.

Trillions – How a Band of Wall Street Renegades Invented the Index Fund and Changed Finance For Ever by **Robin Wigglesworth** (Penguin Random House, 2021): *Financial Times* Journalist Robin Wigglesworth unveils the history of index funds, including ETFs, bringing to life the colourful characters behind their birth, growth and evolution. In doing so it also includes a very comprehensive history of the active vs passive investing debate.

BEHAVIOURAL FINANCE

The Behavior Gap – Simple Ways to Stop Doing Dumb Things with Money by Carl Richards (Penguin Books, 2012): Carl Richards is a US financial planner and creator of the Sketch Guy *New York Times* column, where through his simple sketches he makes complex financial concepts easy to understand. This book includes some of these sketches and teaches the reader how to rein in their own behaviour and stop letting their emotions get in the way of smart financial decisions. There are books by prominent academics that more thoroughly cover the theory of behavioural finance, but *The Behaviour Gap* is practical, easy to follow and focused on personal investing.

ACKNOWLEDGEMENTS

It took a pandemic lockdown and a block of 'gardening leave' that could not be spent travelling that got me to start writing this, but thanks to my daughter Kathryn for the initial inspiration, and to her and her brother David and younger sister Rachel for their help and feedback throughout the process.

Thanks also to my wife, Brenda, for her encouragement, patience and multiple rounds of proofing. To Dr Terence Moll and Dr Graham Beck for their generous and expert feedback on the manuscript. And to Paul Walton and David and Philippa Back for their diligent proof reading of the final draft. Of course, responsibility for any errors in the book remain my own.

And finally, to my former colleague, Ruth Bullivant, who is now a book coach, for her balance of encouragement and challenge to ensure I reworked my original manuscript into a more coherent whole and helped me through to getting this into a publishable book.

ABOUT THE AUTHOR

Walter Coxon has spent 20 years working in the financial services industry, most of that time with the wealth management division of a major banking group. In that time, he held a number of roles, including being head of strategy for the wealth and investment business, on the board of a subsidiary bank and regulated investment firm, head of the firm's global trust business, and COO of a regulated investment firm. While he is not a qualified financial advisor, he is a true wealth industry expert. In 2011 and 2012 he was named by Private Asset Management as one of the '50 Most Influential Private Client Practitioners'. He is now an independent advisor and consultant and on the board of a recently established UK private client trustee firm. In his spare time, he enjoys walking in the countryside and travelling to visit both new and familiar places.

INDEX

ENDNOTES

1   With effect from 1 April 2022.
2   Note I use the term 'portfolios' to include model portfolios (of individual shares and bonds) and funds.
3   "Lloyds-Schroders wealth management venture to launch price war", *Financial Times*, 17 Sept, 2019.
4   Includes initial advice and product charges and annual fees for the 1st year.
5   "*Where Are the Customers' Yachts? or A Good Hard Look at Wall Street*" by Fred Schwed Jr.
6   From The Motley Fool at *https://www.fool.com/investing/general/2014/01/12/warren-buffett-says-this-is-the-worst-investment-y.aspx*
7   Portfolio volatility = $\sqrt{(\sigma_a^2 + \sigma_b^2 + 2r\sigma_a\sigma_b)}$
    Where:
    σ – The volatility of the asset (a or b)
    r – The correlation between (a and b)
8   This paragraph is paraphrased from one similar in "*Winning the Losers Game*" by Charles D Ellis.
9   '*Where the money went in 2020*', Morningstar, 20 January 2021.
10 From Blackrock iShares website *https://www.ishares.com/us/literature/whitepaper/reshaping-sustainable-investing-en-us.pdf*
11 Where your employer makes contributions on a 'salary sacrifice' basis, you actually save another 3.25% in national insurance contributions (from April 2022), so £1 only costs 56.5p.
12 For under 18s there is the 'Junior ISA', with a current savings limit of £9,000 per year.

13   Pension transfer advice: feedback on CP19/25 and final rules and guidance. FCA Policy statement PS20/6, June 2020.

14   The definitions of 'non-domiciled' and 'US person' for UK and US tax purposes are beyond the scope of this book. Generally, if you were born outside of the UK (or even, in some circumstances, have a parent who was born outside of the UK) you could be 'UK non-domiciled'. If you were born in the US or have ever been resident in the US you could well be a US person.

15   BBC, 22 January 2015.

16   https://www.standardlife.co.uk/investments/tools/investment-risk

17   https://www.morningstar.co.uk/uk/news/67084/portfolio-management-for-investors-in-retirement.aspx

18   Actually, you could just buy 'Class B' shares which trade at a much lower price. Class B shares were set up in 1996 to allow retail investors to invest in Berkshire Hathaway, given the high price of the Class A shares.

19   Sum of total assets across both accumulation and income share classes, as of July 2021.

20   Blackrock website.

21   https://www.statista.com/statistics/263435/non-us-share-of-apples-revenue/

22   At time of writing, check these yourself before investing, they do change; it's a competitive market and prices are trending down.

23   Costs from the Lang Cat guide to ISA pricing, March 2020.

24   Real returns include growth and reinvested income and are adjusted for inflation. Data used with kind permission. Copyright © 2021 Elroy Dimson, Paul Marsh and Mike Staunton.

25   Data used with kind permission. Copyright © 2021 Elroy Dimson, Paul Marsh and Mike Staunton.

26   Actually to be precise the real rate of return is 3.92%: $(1+0.06)=(1+0.0393)(1+0.02)$.

27   Yes, of course this is actually 6.08% ($1.04 \times 1.02 = 1.0608$).

28   "*All Your Worth: The Ultimate Lifetime Money Plan*" – Elizabeth Warren and Amelia Warren Tyagi, 2005.

29   The Retail Price Index (RPI) is an inflation metric published by the Office for National Statistics that measures the change in the cost of a representative sample of retail goods and services.

30   "*The beauty of doing nothing*", JPMorgan website article, 26 July 2019.

31   "*There are only two types of investors*" *FT*, 2 July 2020.

32   "*Dalbar QAIB: Investors are Still Their Own Worst Enemies*", IFA.com, 19 April 2021.

33   Not everyone agrees with the methodology behind Dalbar's estimates, which some years have had very high gaps between 'investor returns'

and 'the market'. However, an arguably more rigorous 2007 study by the academic Ilia Dichev (then a professor at the University of Michigan), found an annual gap of around 1.5% for the years of his study, which is close to the Dalbar estimate for the gap to the S&P for 2020.

34 *Nudge*, p34.
35 This view on crypto has been brought to prominence by Jim Cramer, host of Mad Money on CNBC. See https://www.cnbc.com/2021/10/28/cramer-says-speculating-on-crypto-is-ok-as-long-as-investors-know-all-the-risks.html